WAR POEMS

Christopher Martin

Oh war! to them that never tried thee, sweet!
JOSEPH HALL, 1597

The pity of war, the pity war distilled.
WILFRED OWEN, 1918

Collins Educational

An imprint of HarperCollins*Publishers*

Published in 1991 by
Collins Educational
An imprint of HarperCollins*Publishers*
77-85 Fulham Palace Road
London W6 8JB

The HarperCollins website is: www.**fir**eand**water**.com

www.**Collins**Education.com
On-line support for schools and colleges

Reprinted 1992 (twice)
Reprinted 1993 (twice)
Reprinted 1994 (twice)
Reprinted 1995
Reprinted 1996
Reprinted 1997 (twice)
Reprinted 1999 (twice)
Reprinted 2000 (twice)
Reprinted 2001

British Library Cataloguing in Publication Data
War Poems.
   1. Poetry in European languages – Anthologies
   1. Martin, Christopher
   808.81

ISBN 0 00 322238 1

Designed by Linda Reed
Cover illustration: 'The Menin Road' by
Paul Nash, 1919, reproduced by permission of
The Imperial War Museum.

Typeset by Acūté Design Consultants, Stroud
Printed in Great Britain

Contents

Using This Collection

Wilfred Owen's *Dulce et Decorum Est* has become, especially for young readers, the best known of all twentieth century poems. It stands at the centre of this collection of war poetry. Set beside it are familiar, and sometimes very unfamiliar, poems by other male and female poets of the First World War. Some striking and unjustly neglected war poems from the nineteenth century provide a background, while moving poems from the Second World War and afterwards show what has happened to war poetry since 1918.

The poems are arranged in Units which are particularly suitable for GCSE coursework. Units may be studied individually, or several strung together to provide the basis for an extended literary study. There are shorter, specific questions on each poem which may be handled orally or in writing, together with more substantial exercises for written work or discussion, indicated by **W** or **D**. All the written tasks suggested in this book may be used in the GCSE coursework folder: those closely related to the poems will find a place in the English Literature poetry section, while those descriptions and stories more loosely based on poems and pictures will be considered as English work.

The vivid illustrations come from photographic archives and from the impressive War Art collections, and are closely related to the study of the poems. They are therefore an integral part of the book.

CHRISTOPHER MARTIN, 1990

Introduction

War: the glory and the horror

On the Idle Hill

On the idle hill of summer,
  Sleepy with the flow of streams,
Far I hear the steady drummer
  Drumming like a noise in dreams.

Far and near and low and louder
  On the roads of earth go by,
Dear to friends and food for powder,
  Soldiers marching, all to die.

East and west on fields forgotten
  Bleach the bones of comrades slain,
Lovely lads and dead and rotten;
  None that go return again.

Far the calling bugles hollo,
  High the screaming fife replies,
Gay the files of scarlet follow:
  Woman bore me, I will rise.

A.E. HOUSMAN

A.E. Housman was not thinking of a particular war when he wrote this poem in 1896. It is a beautifully balanced general comment on the glamour and the horror of battle. Peace is dull: 'idle' and 'sleepy'. The summons to war has a magnetic attraction with the haunting military music and the hypnotic drum. No young man can resist. Yet the excitement and splendour lead only to death and destruction. Everyone will die, no matter how they are loved, and battlefields and victories are quickly forgotten. Housman sums up what most of us feel about war: it is exciting and fascinating to study but it is also horrible, pointless and mad.

As an introduction to the poems that follow, look at these paired pictures which show contrasting aspects of war.

These pictures are about the battle of Waterloo, fought in June 1815, when British and German troops defeated Napoleon's French army. One is by the Victorian artist, Elizabeth Butler, who specialized in battle scenes. The other is a watercolour of battle-wounded, painted just after the fighting by an army surgeon, Charles Bell.

The Scots' Greys charge at Waterloo: Elizabeth Butler

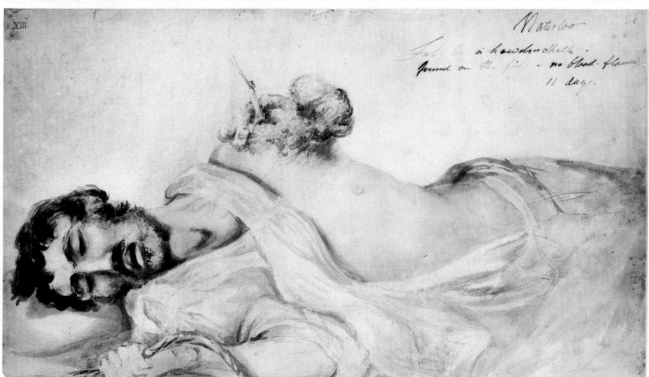

Wounded soldier after Waterloo painted by an army surgeon, Charles Bell

The Guards march through Trafalgar Square on the way to war, 1854

In the Crimean War of 1854-6, both sides were badly organized. W.H. Russell, in his reports to *The Times*, horrified people with his descriptions of the confusion, suffering and waste of life on the British side in the winter of 1854-5.

An officer's sketches of life in the Crimea, winter 1854/5

These contrasting images of women in war date from 1914-18. The first is a recruiting poster, aimed at forcing men to volunteer for the British Army; the second, a drawing by the German artist, Käthe Kollwitz, shows the effect on a woman of news of her husband's death at the Front.

British recruiting poster

Grieving German woman: Käthe Kollwitz

D What do the paired pictures tell us about war, and people's attitudes to it?
What are your own feelings about the pictures?

W Write briefly about each pair of pictures, describing what they tell us about the glamour and horror of war.

Read the following poem.
What is the writer telling us about war?
How does it relate to the pictures that you
have already looked at?

For Two Voices

'O mother, mother, isn't it fun,
    The soldiers marching past in the sun!'
'Child, child, what are you saying?
    Come to church. We should be praying.'

'Look, mother, at their bright spears!'
    'The leaves are falling like women's tears.'
'You are not looking at what I see.'
    'Nay, but I look at what must be.'

'Hark to the pipers! See the flags flying!'
    'I hear the sound of a girl crying.'
'How many hundreds before they are done?'
    'How many mothers wanting a son?'

'Here rides the general, pacing slow!'
    'Well he may, if he knows what I know.'
'O this war, what a glorious game!'
    'Sin and shame, sin and shame.'

            MAURICE HEWLETT, August 1914

W **Make two sets of notes. One should list points**
which make war seem attractive to us
(powerful weapons, uniforms, stories of
courage, film images, etc.); the other should
list points which make war horrific to us (death
and wounds, waste of resources, killing of
children, destruction, etc.).

D **Hold a discussion about people's attitudes to**
war in the late twentieth century and in
history. Use your notes as a basis for the
debate.

— PART 1 —

The Napoleonic era to the Boer War

War poetry brings history to life by telling us the private thoughts of men and women who have experienced conflict between nations. Today many young people find that the work of the soldier poets of 1914-18 is the most impressive part of the huge literature of war. There were no soldier poets before the end of the nineteenth century. The endless battles were fought by illiterate men whose thoughts are lost to us. War poets were civilians who, although they might have seen army service, mostly used their imagination to say what battle was like.

The chaos of a seventeenth-century battle: there were no soldier poets to describe what the fighting was like

UNIT 1   *War against Napoleon*

The long series of struggles (1792-1815) between revolutionary France and rival European powers made up the first modern 'total war'. Not only were there huge armies in the field and great fleets at sea but also journalists were able to stir up civilian populations to patriotic fury:

Secure from actual warfare, we have loved
To swell the war-whoop, passionate for war! . . .
                    . . . Boys and girls,
And women, that would groan to see a child
Pull off an insect's leg, all read of war,
The best amusement for our morning meal! . . .
As if the soldier died without a wound, . . .
As though he had no wife to pine for him. . . .

                    S.T.COLERIDGE, from *Fears in Solitude* 1798

However, many people admired the ideals of liberty and equality which were produced by the French Revolution and this resulted in strong anti-war writing.

John Scott was a Quaker and therefore opposed to all violence. He wrote *The Drum* (see the next page) in 1782 but it remained very popular and was reprinted many times during the Napoleonic era. For centuries what Shakespeare called the 'spirit-stirring drum' had been used by recruiting officers to attract men into the Army.

John Bull's progress: *James Gillray, 1793*

JOHN BULL Happy.

JOHN BULL going to the WARS.

JOHN BULL'S Property in danger.

JOHN BULL'S glorious Return.

JOHN BULL'S *PROGRESS.*

The Drum

I hate that drum's discordant sound,
Parading round, and round, and round:
To thoughtless youth it pleasure yields,
And lures from cities and from fields,
To sell their liberty for charms
Of tawdry[1] lace, and glittering arms;
And when Ambition's voice commands,
To march, and fight, and fall, in foreign lands.

I hate that drum's discordant sound,
Parading round, and round, and round:
To me it talks of ravaged plains,
And burning towns, and ruined swains,[2]
And mangled limbs, and dying groans,
And widows' tears,and orphans' moans;
And all that Misery's hand bestows,
To fill the catalogue of human woes.

JOHN SCOTT

[1] showy (lace was used in officers' uniforms)
[2] young men

What pictures of the attractive side of army life does the drum produce in young men's minds?
What is the key word in the first verse?
What grim details of war does the drum produce in Scott's mind?
What is the key word in the second verse?
How does the rhythm of the poem imitate the sound of the drum?
The poem has been admired for the perfect balance of its verses. Do you agree?
The last line in each verse is longer than the others. What is effective about this?

W Write about the poem, outlining its main ideas and saying what you find interesting in the way it is written.

W Study the cartoon, *John Bull's progress (on p.11),* by James Gillray. It has roughly the same theme as *The Drum.* Write descriptively or imaginatively about what is happening in each picture. Say how the cartoon is like the poem and which you find more impressive.

Robert Southey wrote *The Battle of Blenheim* in 1798, looking back to 1704 when the Duke of Marlborough defeated the French and Austrians. The poem was intended to support the pressure against a war with France in 1798. (Old Kaspar is a peasant who lives on the former battlefield.)

The Battle of Blenheim

I

It was a summer evening,
　Old Kaspar's work was done,
And he before his cottage door
　Was sitting in the sun,
And by him sported on the green
His little grandchild Wilhelmine.

II

She saw her brother Peterkin
　Roll something large and round,
Which he beside the rivulet
　In playing there had found;
He came to ask what he had found,
That was so large, and smooth, and round.

III

Old Kaspar took it from the boy,
　Who stood expectant by;
And then the old man shook his head,
　And, with a natural sigh,
' 'Tis some poor fellow's skull,' said he,
'Who fell in the great victory.

IV

'I find them in the garden,
　For there's many here about;
And often when I go to plough,
　The ploughshare turns them out!
For many thousand men,' said he,
'Were slain in that great victory.'

V

'Now tell us what 'twas all about,'
　Young Peterkin, he cries;
And little Wilhelmine looks up
　With wonder-waiting eyes;
'Now tell us all about the war,
And what they fought each other for.'

VI

'It was the English,' Kaspar cried,
　'Who put the French to rout;
But what they fought each other for,
　I could not well make out;
But everybody said,' quoth he,
'That 'twas a famous victory.

VII

'My father lived at Blenheim then,
　Yon little stream hard by;
They burnt his dwelling to the ground,
　And he was forced to fly;
So with his wife and child he fled,
Nor had he where to rest his head.

VIII

'With fire and sword the country round
  Was wasted far and wide,
And many a childing mother then,
  And new-born baby died;
But things like that, you know, must be
At every famous victory.

IX

'They say it was a shocking sight
  After the field was won;
For many thousand bodies here
  Lay rotting in the sun;
But things like that, you know, must be
After a famous victory.

X

'Great praise the Duke of Marlbro' won,
  And our good Prince Eugene.'[1]
'Why 'twas a very wicked thing!'
  Said little Wilhelmine.
'Nay . . . nay . . . my little girl,' quoth he,
'It was a famous victory.

XI

'And everybody praised the Duke
  Who this great fight did win.'
'But what good came of it at last?'
  Quoth little Peterkin.
'Why that I cannot tell,' said he
'But 'twas a famous victory.'

ROBERT SOUTHEY

[1] the Allied commanders

**What starts the discussion of the Battle?
Old Kaspar recalls gruesome details of the
fighting. What are these? What does he not
understand about it?
What do the children want to know?
What are their opinions after Old Kaspar's
account?
Do you find the use of the children effective
here? Why?
Do you like the simple style of the poem?
Is it as simple as it looks?
Where is it most powerful?
What does the poem tell us about the horror
and futility of war?**

W **Write your own conversation between
modern children and their grandfather, who
is telling them about a war in our century that
he remembers. Perhaps they start by looking
at something from the war: medals, a photo,
an old shell case. Base the argument closely
on** *Blenheim* **so that you put across the same
message about war.**

The night before Waterloo

Lord Byron, writing just after the great battle in
1815, brilliantly recreated the fear and excitement
of Brussels on the eve of the fighting.

  . . . the beat of the alarming drum
    Roused up the soldier ere the morning star;
    While thronged the citizens with terror dumb,
Or whispering, with white lips – 'The foe! They come!
  They come!'

LORD BYRON, *Childe Harold*, Canto 3, 1816

Later in the nineteenth century, the German poet,
Rainer Maria Rilke, looked back on the same night.
He imagined a young officer saying goodbye to his
wife before he went into battle. (The German
Brunswicker – Prussian – troops fought under
Wellington's command. They wore a black
plumed hat, a *shako*, grimly decorated with a
skull-and-crossbones badge.)

Before Waterloo, the Last Night

And night and muffled creakings and the wheels
of the artillery-wagons circling with the clock,
Blücher's[1] Prussian army passing the estate. . . .
The man plays the harpsichord,[2] and lifts his eyes,
playing each air by ear to look at her –
he might be looking in a mirror for himself,
a mirror filled with his young face, the sorrow
his music made seductive and beautiful.
Suddenly everything is over. Instead,
wearily by an open window, she stands
and clasps the helpless thumping of her heart.
No sound. Outside, a fresh morning wind has risen,
and strangely foreign on the mirror-table,
leans his black shako with its white deathshead.

RAINER MARIA RILKE (translated by Robert Lowell)

[1] field-marshal
[2] piano-like instrument

**What is the scene? What is the mood? What is
happening outside?**

Why are the couple speechless? What do you imagine are their thoughts?

Why is the man playing the harpsichord? How do the silence and the morning wind change the mood at the end?

What do man and woman think of as they look at the black shako in the last line?

W Write about the poem. First describe the room and what is in it. Mention the sounds that make the atmosphere. Give the thoughts of the man and the thoughts and fears of the woman. End with the couple looking in horror at the death's head badge on the shako just before the man leaves for battle.

Shako

UNIT 2 *The Crimean War 1854–6*

Britain and France feared Russia's ambition to spread its power southwards as the Turkish Empire collapsed. War broke out in 1854. In September, the Allies landed in the Crimea, in southern Russia, and besieged Sebastopol. In October the Russians attacked the British base at Balaclava.

During this battle, the disastrous Charge of the Light Brigade took place. The British cavalry commander mistook his orders to retake some guns held by the Russians. Instead he told his men to charge the main Russian position, which was at the head of a valley bristling with artillery. The 600 horsemen gallantly obeyed but two thirds of the force were killed or wounded. The Charge is the best known example of the heroism and stupidity of war.

W.H. Russell, a correspondent for *The Times*, became famous for his reports from the Crimea. This is how he described the Charge.

At ten minutes past eleven our Light Cavalry Brigade advanced . . . .They swept proudly past, glittering in the morning sun in all the pride and splendour of war. . . . At the distance of 1,200 yards the whole line of the enemy belched forth, from thirty iron mouths, a flood of smoke and flame. The flight was marked by instant gaps in our ranks, by dead men and horses, by steeds flying wounded or riderless across the plain. In diminished ranks, with a halo of steel above their heads, and with a cheer which was many a noble fellow's death cry, they flew into the smoke of the batteries; but ere they were lost from view the plain was strewn with their bodies. Through the clouds of smoke we could see their sabres flashing as they rode between the guns, cutting down the gunners as they stood. We saw them riding through, returning, after breaking through a column of Russians and scattering them like chaff, when the flank fire of the batteries on the hill swept them down. Wounded men and dismounted troopers flying towards us told the sad tale . . . at thirty-five minutes past eleven not a British soldier, except the dead and the dying, was left in front of the Muscovite guns.

The Times, 14 November 1854

Alfred Tennyson read the report and wrote
this poem very quickly as a result.

The Charge of the Light Brigade

I
Half a league, half a league,
  Half a league onward,
All in the valley of Death
  Rode the six hundred.
'Forward, the Light Brigade!
Charge for the guns!' he said:
Into the valley of Death
  Rode the six hundred.

II
'Forward, the Light Brigade!'
Was there a man dismayed?
Not though the soldier knew
  Some one had blundered:
Their's not to make reply,
Their's not to reason why,
Their's but to do and die:
Into the valley of Death
  Rode the six hundred.

III
Cannon to right of them,
Cannon to left of them,
Cannon in front of them
  Volleyed and thundered;
Stormed at with shot and shell,
Boldly they rode and well,
Into the jaws of Death,
Into the mouth of Hell
  Rode the six hundred.

IV
Flashed all their sabres bare,
Flashed as they turned in air
Sabring the gunners there,

Charging an army, while
  All the world wondered:
Plunged in the battery-smoke
Right through the line they broke;
Cossack and Russian
Reeled from the sabre-stroke
  Shattered and sundered.
Then they rode back, but not
  Not the six hundred.

V
Cannon to right of them,
Cannon to left of them,
Cannon behind them
  Volleyed and thundered;
Stormed at with shot and shell,
While horse and hero fell,
They that had fought so well
Came through the jaws of Death,
Back from the mouth of Hell,
All that was left of them,
  Left of six hundred.

VI
When can their glory fade?
O the wild charge they made!
  All the world wondered.
Honour the charge they made!
Honour the Light Brigade,
  Noble six hundred!

ALFRED TENNYSON

The poem has a wonderful rhythm. What is it
imitating?
Which line tells you a mistake had been
made?
What does Tennyson mean by:
  Their's not to reason why,
  Their's but to do and die: . . . ?
Which details from Russell's report does
Tennyson borrow?

Where does Tennyson show his admiration
and his pity for the soldiers?
What, finally, do you think that he felt about
the Charge?

Compare the newspaper report and the poem.
Which do you prefer? Why?

W Look at these contrasting pictures. Write about the Charge, using ideas and details from the report, the poem, and the two pictures. You may perhaps imagine yourself as one of the few survivors.

The Charge of the Light Brigade: *Caton Woodville*

After the Charge: *Elizabeth Butler*

UNIT 3   *The American Civil War 1861–5*

The ferocious war between the Northern Union states and the Southern Confederacy began in June 1861. The North, led by President Lincoln, wished to end slavery; the South resisted fiercely and decided to leave the Union. The Northern victory in the bloody battle of Gettysburg, in July 1863, was the turning-point that led to the final defeat of the South in 1865.

The great American poet, Walt Whitman, soon lost his early enthusiasm for the Civil War. He worked as a 'wound dresser', tending battle victims in primitive camp hospitals. He recorded the horror and suffering that he saw there in his fine poems, *Drum Taps*. Here Whitman writes imaginatively about the effects of war on a farming family (Ohio was on the Northern side). A letter from the front tells them bad news about their son, Pete.

Come up from the Fields Father

Come up from the fields father, here's a letter from our
    Pete,
And come to the front door mother, here's a letter from
    thy dear son.

Lo, 'tis autumn,
Lo, where the trees, deeper green, yellower and redder,
Cool and sweeten Ohio's villages with leaves fluttering
    in the moderate wind,

Where apples ripe in the orchards hang and grapes on
    the trellis'd vines,
(Smell you the smell of the grapes on the vines?
Smell you the buckwheat where the bees were lately
    buzzing?)

Above all, lo, the sky so calm, so transparent after the
    rain, and with wondrous clouds,
Below too, all calm, all vital and beautiful, and the farm
    prospers well.

Down in the fields all prospers well,
But now from the fields come father, come at the
    daughter's call,
And come to the entry mother, to the front door come
    right away.

Fast as she can she hurries, something ominous, her
    steps trembling,
She does not tarry to smooth her hair nor adjust her cap.

Open the envelope quickly,
O this is not our son's writing, yet his name is sign'd,
O a strange hand writes for our dear son, O stricken
    mother's soul!
All swims before her eyes, flashes with black, she
    catches the main words only,
Sentences broken, *gunshot wound in the breast, cavalry
    skirmish, taken to hospital,*
At present low, but will soon be better.

Ah now the single figure to me,
Amid all teeming and wealthy Ohio with all its cities
    and farms,
Sickly white in the face and dull in the head, very faint,
By the jamb of a door leans.

Grieve not so, dear mother, (the just-grown daughter
    speaks through her sobs,
The little sisters huddle around speechless and
    dismay'd,)
See, dearest mother, the letter says Pete will soon be better.

Alas poor boy, he will never be better, (nor may-be
    needs to be better, that brave and simple soul,)
While they stand at home at the door he is dead already,
The only son is dead.

But the mother needs to be better,
She with thin form presently drest in black,
By day her meals untouch'd, then at night fitfully
    sleeping, often waking,
In the midnight waking, weeping, longing with one
    deep longing,
O that she might withdraw unnoticed, silent from life
    escape and withdraw,
To follow, to seek, to be with her dear dead son.

WALT WHITMAN

Why does Whitman write about the beauties of the farm, the landscape and the sky? What contrast does this make with the news about Pete? How do his choice of words, short sentences and punctuation create the effect of nervousness and shock in the mother? As the daughter tries to console her mother, Whitman adds a bitter twist to the story. What is this?

In another poem, Whitman wrote these lines about the battle dead:

I saw battle corpses, myriads of them,
And the white skeletons of young men – I saw
    them . . .
But I saw they were not as was thought;
They themselves were fully at rest – they suffer'd
    not;
The living remain'd and suffer'd – the mother
    suffer'd,
And the wife and the child, and the musing
    comrade suffer'd . . .

Why are these lines like the last section of *Come up from the Fields Father?*

W Imagine that you are one of this family. Tell the story of the poem through that person's eyes. Include more details of the family and the farm, and of the feelings and reactions of the family to the news. Also include Whitman's ideas about the beautiful Ohio landscape.

W The first dramatic photographs of battle were taken during the American Civil War. Tell the story of this soldier (right), perhaps through the eyes of a close army friend. You could make him into Pete of the poem.

The Civil War cost the lives of more than half a million men on the two sides. Bret Harte, a journalist and short story writer, found a strange new way to think about these deaths in a poem.

What the Bullet Sang

O joy of creation
        To be!
O rapture to fly
        And be free!
Be the battle lost or won,
Though its smoke shall hide the sun,
I shall find my love, – the one
        Born for me!

I shall know him where he stands,
        All alone,
With the power in his hands
        Not o'erthrown;
I shall know him by his face,
By his godlike front and grace;
I shall hold him for a space,
        All my own!

It is he – O my love!
        So bold!
It is I – all thy love
        Foretold!
It is I. O love! What bliss!
Dost thou answer to my kiss?
O sweetheart! What is this
        Lieth there so cold?

BRET HARTE

**This looks like a love poem
but it is not.
What is it about?
Who is the 'speaker'?
Do you find the poem comic/sad/bitter/
horrifying?
What is the point of these words:**
    Born for me!
    . . . his godlike front and grace;
What is this Lieth there so cold? . . . ?
**Do you find the poem impressive or merely
strange?**

*Dead Confederate soldier at Fredricksburg, 1863:
Photographed by Timothy O'Sullivan*

UNIT 4   *Defending the Empire*

Pride in the vast British Empire was an important part of the life and thought of late-Victorian Britain, not least in the great independent public schools. There the men were reared who would rule and lead the fight to defend the overseas possessions. Latin and Greek were still the basis of study in these schools, and lessons from the

writers of Rome were eagerly seized upon to guide the new Empire builders. The Roman poet Lucretius had such a message:

Some nations grow and others fade and in a short space of time the generations of living things change and, like runners, hand on the torch of life . . .

British army machine-gun detachment, 1895

Henry Newbolt was the most patriotic poet of Britain's Empire. He borrowed Lucretius' idea to make the title of his 1892 poem, *Vitai Lampada:* the torch of life. He begins with boys playing cricket in a public school. Then he sees them as men defending some outpost of Empire.

Vitai Lampada

There's a breathless hush in the Close tonight –
    Ten to make and the match to win –
A bumping pitch and a blinding light,
    An hour to play and the last man in.
And it's not for the sake of a ribboned coat,
    Or the selfish hope of a season's fame,
But his Captain's hand on his shoulder smote:
    'Play up! play up! and play the game!'

The sand of the desert is sodden red, –
  Red with the wreck of a square[1] that broke; –
The Gatling's[2] jammed and the Colonel dead,
  And the regiment blind with dust and smoke.
The river of death has brimmed his banks,
  And England's far, and Honour a name,
But the voice of a schoolboy rallies the ranks:
  'Play up! play up! and play the game!'

This is the word that year by year,
  While in her place the School is set,
Every one of her sons must hear,
  And none that hears it dare forget.
This they all with a joyful mind
  Beat through life like a torch in flame,
And, falling, fling to the host behind –
  'Play up! play up! and play the game!'

                              HENRY NEWBOLT

[1] military formation
[2] machine gun

What is the boys' situation in the first verse?
What is the Captain's message?
What is happening in the second verse?
What is strange about the officer's call?
What message does Newbolt have for public school boys in the last verse?

What exactly is the torch that they hand on?
Do you find this poem exciting/ memorable/ outdated/ridiculous/inspiring?
How is war seen in this poem?
Compare it to this passage from a famous war correspondent's report for the *Daily Mail*, **describing Kitchener's army in the Sudan:**

The bullets had whispered to raw youngsters in one breath the secret of all the glories of the British Army. . . . Three men went down without a cry at the very foot of the Union Jack. . . . The flag shook itself and still blazed splendidly . . . don't look too much about you. Black spindle-legs curled up to meet red-gimleted black faces, donkeys headless and legless or sieves of shrapnel, camels . . . rotting already in pools of blood . . . heads without faces and faces without anything below . . . don't look at it all. . . . Once more, hurrah, hurrah, hurrah . . .

George Steevens: *Daily Mail*, April 1898

W **Write a letter to Henry Newbolt telling him what you like and what you dislike about his poem and the ideas that it contains. Quote from the poem to support your points either way.**

UNIT 5   *The Boer War 1899-1902*

The Boer War began as a struggle between British and Dutch 'Boer' settlers for control of diamond and gold deposits in the Orange Free State and Transvaal. After early defeats, the British Army, reinforced by troops from other parts of the Empire, claimed victory in 1900. However, the Boers, who were great horse-riders and riflemen, continued fighting by using clever guerilla tactics. Only when the British adopted a 'scorched earth' policy, whereby farms were burned and women and children were rounded up into 'concentration camps', did they finally crush the Boers.

The spread of education in the nineteenth century had produced a flood of popular newspapers and magazines. Poetry about the fighting in South Africa was a feature of these during the Boer War. There was some crude verse from soldiers but the most impressive poems came from war correspondents at the front or from civilians at home. As there was much opposition to the purpose and methods of the conflict, anti-war verse was a striking feature of this writing.

Death on the veldt: comparing two poems

Thomas Hardy, already famous for his novels, wrote some of the best poems of the War. His powerful imagination allowed him to share the feelings and experiences of people more actively involved.

In his local Dorset newspaper, Hardy read of the death of a drummer boy, who was born in a village near Dorchester. He thought how sad it was that a boy, too young to understand the war, should be buried in an alien landscape so far from home. 'Hodge' was a nickname given at that time to the typical 'country bumpkin'. Hardy usually objected to the name but used it here to show the cruelty of war to the individual.

Drummer Hodge

They throw in Drummer Hodge, to rest
    Uncoffined – just as found:
His landmark is a kopje-crest[1]
    That breaks the veldt [2] around;
And foreign constellations west
    Each night above his mound.

Young Hodge the Drummer never knew –
    Fresh from his Wessex home –
The meaning of the broad Karoo,[3]
    The Bush, the dusty loam,
And why uprose to nightly view
    Strange stars amid the gloam.[4]

Yet portion of that unknown plain
    Will Hodge for ever be;
His homely Northern breast and brain
    Grow to some southern tree,
And strange-eyed constellations reign
    His stars eternally.

THOMAS HARDY

[1] small hill
[2] open grassland
[3] dry uplands
[4] evening

What is the force of these words and phrases:
They . . . throw in . . . uncoffined . . . ?
What did Hodge never understand during his war service in South Africa?
Hardy uses several South African words. Why? What effect do they have on the theme of the poem?
Why does Hardy find Hodge's fate more strange than tragic?
What does Hardy mean in the last verse by:
His homely Northern breast and brain
    Grow to some southern tree, . . .?

'Thrown in, just as found': British dead at Spion Kop, January 1900

The silence of Hodge in death is an important part of Hardy's poem. B. Paul Neuman, another Boer War poet, allows his dead soldiers to speak their thoughts in his *Vox Militantis* (The Voice of the Soldier).

Vox Militantis

On the wide veldt, beneath the vaster sky,
The graves of battling Boer and Briton lie.
By day the sunlight watches o'er their sleep,
By night the stars their solemn vigil[1] keep.

Cold, calm, and brilliant, from that awful height
They ask: 'Were ye so weary of the light?
Ours the slow aeons,[2] yours the flying day,
Why reckless fling its noon and eve away?'

And lo, the answer: 'Nay, but life was sweet,
Death a grim horror that we loathed to meet,
But Duty spurred us to the foremost place,
And Honour beckoned with a shining face.'

B. PAUL NEUMAN

[1] watch
[2] ages

W **Write about the two poems, saying how they are alike and how they differ.**
Look at the poets' ideas and use of language.
What contrasting thoughts about war do they offer?
Which do you think is the better poem?

UNIT 6   *Pictures from the Boer War*

Thomas Hardy's *A Wife in London* describes a lonely woman waiting nervously for news of her husband fighting in South Africa, the 'far South Land'.

A Wife in London

I

She sits in the tawny vapour
    That the Thames-side lanes have uprolled,
    Behind whose webby fold on fold
Like a waning taper
    The street-lamp glimmers cold.

A messenger's knock cracks smartly,
    Flashed news is in her hand
    Of meaning it dazes to understand
Though shaped so shortly:
    He–has fallen–in the far South Land. . . .

II

'Tis the morrow; the fog hangs thicker,
    The postman nears and goes:
    A letter is brought whose lines disclose
By the firelight flicker
    His hand, whom the worm now knows:

Fresh – firm – penned in highest feather –
    Page-full of his hoped return,
    And of home-planned jaunts by brake and burn
In the summer weather,
    And of new love that they would learn.

THOMAS HARDY

What might the woman be thinking as she sits at home?
What do the fog and the street lamp seem to represent to her?
Hardy was always impressed by twists of fate in people's lives. What grim joke does fate play on the woman in part II of the poem?

Edgar Wallace was a medical orderly in South Africa when the war began. Later he became a war correspondent. He blended his knowledge of the horrible effects of battle with the vivid style of the journalist in his poem *War*.

War

I

A tent that is pitched at the base:
    A wagon that comes from the night:
A stretcher–and on it a Case:
    A surgeon, who's holding a light,
The Infantry's bearing the brunt –
    O hark to the wind-carried cheer!
A mutter of guns at the front:
    A whimper of sobs at the rear.
And it's *War*! 'Orderly, hold the light.
    You can lay him down on the table: so.
Easily – gently! Thanks – you may go.'
    And it's *War*! but the part that is not for show.

II

A tent, with a table athwart,
    A table that's laid out for one;

A waterproof cover – and nought
　But the limp, mangled work of a gun.
A bottle that's stuck by the pole,
　A guttering dip in its neck;
The flickering light of a soul
　On the wondering eyes of The Wreck,[1]
And it's *War*! 'Orderly, hold his hand.
　I'm not going to hurt you, so don't be afraid.
A ricochet![2] God! what a mess it has made!'
　And it's *War*! and a very unhealthy trade.

III

The clink of a stopper and glass:
　A sigh as the chloroform drips:
A trickle of – what? on the grass,
　And bluer and bluer the lips.
The lashes have hidden the stare . . .
　A rent, and the clothes fall away . . .
A touch, and the wound is laid bare . . .
　A cut, and the face has turned grey . . .
And it's *War*! 'Orderly, take It out.
　It's hard for his child, and it's rough on his wife.
There might have been – sooner – a chance for his life
　But it's *War*! And – Orderly, clean this knife!'

EDGAR WALLACE

[1] wounded man
[2] a rebound bullet

Wallace tells us what the orderly *hears* **as well as what he sees. Which sounds add to the drama and atmosphere of the poem?**
　What does he mean by:
　　War! but the part that is not for show. . .?
What is the effect of these phrases:
　　. . . a very unhealthy trade.
　　'Orderly, clean this knife!' . . .?
What is 'It' in the last verse and why is the word so sinister?

Rudyard Kipling, who was already world famous as a poet and novelist, went to South Africa as a reporter. Usually he was a devoted supporter of the military and of the British Empire but he had moments of grave doubt as he watched the effects of the war.

He deeply respected the women who followed in the tradition of Florence Nightingale by volunteering for war service as nurses. His phrase describing young women who died – 'little wasted bodies' – reminds us that a large proportion of Boer War casualties were caused by disease rather than battle.

An army surgeon tends the wounded in the field at Colenso, 1899

Dirge of the Dead Sisters

(For the Nurses who died in the South African War)

Who recalls the twilight and the ranged tents in order
(Violet peaks uplifted through the crystal evening air)?
And the clink of iron teacups and the piteous, noble
   laughter,
And the faces of the Sisters with the dust upon their
   hair? . . .

Who recalls the noontide and the funerals through the
   market
(Blanket-hidden bodies, flagless, followed by the flies)?
And the footsore firing-party, and the dust and stench
   and staleness,
And the faces of the Sisters and the glory in their eyes?

(Bold behind the battle, in the open camp all-hallowed,
Patient, wise and mirthful in the ringed and reeking
   town,
These endured unresting till they rested from their
   labours –
Little wasted bodies, ah, so light to lower down)!

RUDYARD KIPLING

**Which details in the poem stress the vividness
of life during the war?
What does Kipling particularly admire about
the nurses and their work?
What is the second verse about? Which word
contrasts with the depressing detail there?
What is the force of the word 'light' in the last
line?**

In *The Hyaenas*, Kipling notes how these ugly
Bush scavengers would dig up and eat newly
buried soldiers.

The Hyaenas

After the burial-parties leave
   And the baffled kites have fled;
The wise hyaenas come out at eve
   To take account of our dead.

How he died and why he died
   Troubles them not a whit.
They snout the bushes and stones aside
   And dig till they come to it.

They are only resolute they shall eat
   That they and their mates may thrive,
And they know the dead are safer meat
   Than the weakest thing alive.

(For a goat may butt, and a worm may sting,
   And a child will sometimes stand;
But a poor dead soldier of the King
   Can never lift a hand.)

They whoop and halloo and scatter the dirt
   Until their tushes white
Take good hold in the army shirt,
   And tug the corpse to light,

And the pitiful face is shewn again
   For an instant ere they close;
But it is not discovered to living men –
   Only to God and to those

Who, being soulless, are free from shame,
   Whatever meat they may find.
Nor do they defile the dead man's name –
   That is reserved for his kind.

RUDYARD KIPLING

**Which words and phrases express horror at
the hyaenas and their behaviour?
Which express understanding of them?
What is the force of the first two lines of the
second verse?
Why is the fourth verse so pathetic?
What deadly, angry point is Kipling making
in the last two lines?**

W **Look over the four poems:** *A Wife in London,
War, Dirge of the Dead Sisters,* **and** *The Hyaenas.*
**They describe the pity of war in South Africa.
Write about the poems, saying what each is
about. Mention anything striking that you
find in the ideas or the language of the poems.
End by saying which poem you find most
impressive.**

UNIT 7 *Looking forward to war*

In the early years of the twentieth century, the possibility of a war in Europe was much discussed. The continent became divided by great alliances: Britain, France and Russia against Germany and Austria-Hungary. Large armies were built up and battle plans worked out. There were flash points in the Balkans and colonial rivalries which increased the tension. William Watson, in his poem *The World in Armour*, drew an ominous picture of

The Europe of the present, as she stands
Powerless from terror of her own vast power,
And round her the sad kings, with sleepless hands
Piling the faggots, hour by doomful hour. . . .

Battleships were the most impressive weapon systems before 1914. Britain and Germany were caught in a deadly race to produce more of these 'floating steel castles'. In the following poem, Thomas Hardy starts with the sound of battleships practice-firing their guns at sea.

Channel Firing

That night your great guns, unawares,
Shook all our coffins as we lay,
And broke the chancel window-squares,
We thought it was the Judgement-day

And sat upright. While drearisome
Arose the howl of wakened hounds:
The mouse let fall the altar-crumb,
The worms drew back into the mounds,

The glebe cow drooled. Till God called, 'No;
It's gunnery practice out at sea
Just as before you went below;
The world is as it used to be:

'All nations striving strong to make
Red war yet redder. Mad as hatters
They do no more for Christés sake
Than you who are helpless in such matters.

'That this is not the judgement-hour
For some of them's a blessed thing,
For if it were they'd have to scour
Hell's floor for so much threatening . . .

'Ha, ha. It will be warmer when
I blow the trumpet (if indeed
I ever do; for you are men,
And rest eternal sorely need).'

So down we lay again, 'I wonder,
Will the world ever saner be,'
Said one, 'than when He sent us under
In our indifferent century!'

And many a skeleton shook his head,
'Instead of preaching forty year,'
My neighbour Parson Thirdly said,
'I wish I had stuck to pipes and beer.'

Again the guns disturbed the hour,
Roaring their readiness to avenge,
As far inland as Stourton Tower,
And Camelot, and starlit Stonehenge.

THOMAS HARDY

The War, *by Arnold Bocklin (1896), shows the Four Horsemen of the Apocalypse – violence, famine, disease, and death – who represent symbolically the effects of war*

'We' are dead men lying in coffins in the vaults of a church.

Why do they sit up?

What is the heart of God's message to them?

What is the state of the world when the dead men wake?

What discussion do the skeletons have at the end?

To what conclusion do they come?

Do you find this poem comic/serious/frightening?

Do you think it is now out of date, or has it something to tell us about our world?

W Write your own sketch, based loosely on the ideas of this poem. The dead are awoken by some warlike sounds from today (aircraft perhaps) and question you about war and peace in the late twentieth century.

— PART 2 —

The First World War 1914-18

Introduction: *The trench world*

Repelling a German counter-attack, *by Frank Dadd, shows typical 1914-18 warfare with heavy infantry losses during attacks on lines defended by barbed-wire and machine-guns*

from: **In the Dordogne**

And each day one died or another
Died: each week we sent out thousands
That returned by hundreds
Wounded or gassed. . . .
　　　　JOHN PEALE BISHOP, 1918

The Western Front was a maze of trenches
stretching 720 kilometres across Europe from
Switzerland to the Belgian coast. It was created
after the failure of the Germans to defeat France
quickly, as they had planned to do, by sweeping
through Belgium to capture Paris. In September
1914, Britain and France held this advance at the
decisive Battle of the Marne, and pushed back the
Germans. As winter approached, both sides dug
defensive lines of trenches. These were extended
northward during the 'race to the sea' of late-1914.
Both sides paused to rebuild their forces and the
trenches were developed into a vast complex of
ditches.

> All the spectacular side of war was gone, never to
> reappear . . . trenches and always trenches and
> nothing showing above the surface of the ground.
> Day after day the butchery of the unknown by the
> unseen . . .
>
> 　　　　　*The Times*, 24 November 1914

Until 1918, the line seemed impossible to break.
The mighty artillery ruled the battlefields.

We are the guns, and your masters! Saw ye our flashes?
Heard ye the scream of our shells in the night, and the
　　shuddering crashes?
Saw ye our work at the roadside, the shrouded things
　　lying,
Moaning to God that He made them, the maimed and
　　the dying?
Husbands or sons,
Fathers or lovers, we break them. We are the guns!
　　　　GILBERT FRANKAU, from *The Guns*, 1917

However, it was the weapons of defence, the
barbed wire and the machine-gun, that held up
and cut down would-be attackers and that
produced the trench stalemate of 1915-18.

The ideal trench was 2 metres (6 feet) deep with
sandbag parapets, fire-steps for sentries, and
wooden duck-boards laid over drainage channels.
Few trenches were ideal. Some seemed to be built
of the men who had died defending them.

> Every square yard of ground seemed to be layered
> with corpses, producing a sickening stench. We
> would curtain off protruding parts with a sand-bag,
> pinned to the side of the trench with cartridges. A
> swollen right arm, with a German eagle tattooed on it,
> used to stick out and brush us as we squeezed by . . .
>
> 　　George Coppard, from *With a Machine-gun to Cambrai*

The power of the artillery:
War drawing no.2:
P. Wyndham Lewis

A tangle of trenches near Loos, 1915; intense fighting is marked by white chalk thrown up by shell bursts

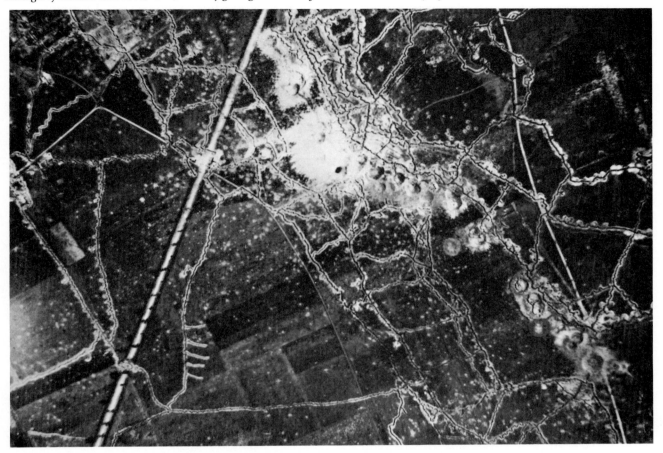

Dense barbed-wire defences: German lines at Beaurevoir, 1918

Rain, mud, rats, lice, and tiredness, fear and boredom were the daily realities of trench life. There were months of tedium.

> No sign of humanity . . . a dead land. And yet thousands of men were there, like rabbits concealed. The artillery was quiet; there was no sound but a cuckoo in a shell-torn poplar. Then, as a rabbit in the early morning comes out to crop grass, a German stepped over the enemy trench – the only living thing in sight. 'I'll take him,' says the man near me. And like a rabbit the German falls . . .
>
> Ivar Campbell, from a letter, 1915

A raid across No Man's Land, between the trench lines, to attack the enemy released furious violence.

> The British flung in on top of the defenders like terriers into a rat pit, and the fighters snarled and worried and scuffled and clutched and tore at each other more like savage brutes than men. The defence was not broken or driven out – it was killed out; and lunging bayonet and smashing butt caught and finished the few that tried to struggle and claw a way out of the slippery trench sides.
>
> Boyd Cable, from *Between the Lines*

Over the top: the crisis point of trench war when soldiers jumped over the parapet to attack the enemy lines

The British war effort was dominated by the vast battles of the Somme (1916) and Ypres (1917), which lasted for months, involved millions of men, and absorbed thousands of lives. The artist Paul Nash painted the hideous battlefields around Ypres and wrote an angry protest about them in a letter home.

> The rain drives on, the stinking mud becomes more evilly yellow, the shell-holes fill up with green-white water . . . the black, dying trees ooze and sweat and the shells never cease . . . annihilating, maiming, maddening they plunge into the grave which is this land; one huge grave and cast upon it the poor dead. It is unspeakable, godless, hopeless . . .
>
> Paul Nash, November 1917

The Harvest of Battle, *by C.R.W. Nevinson, shows the horrific wasteland made by endless trench warfare*

War poetry 1914-18

The fashion for war poetry of the Boer War era was revived in 1914. The press was once again filled with poems, often used to stimulate recruiting or to comment on war news. Most of this early war verse was very bad.

At the sound of the drum
Out of their dens they come, they come,
The little poets we hoped were dumb
The little poets we hoped were dead
The poets who certainly haven't been read
Since heaven knows when, they come, they come,
At the sound of the drum, of the drum, of the drum . . .

Anonymous poem, 1914

The death of Rupert Brooke and the craze for his war sonnets (see p.36) began a second fashion for 'soldier poets'. Many young officers strung together verses about Honour, Duty, and Sacrifice. As the men fell in battle, proud parents published these 'poems' in slim volumes.

> Lying about in every smart London drawing-room, you would find the latest little volume, and at every fashionable bookshop the half-crown war poets were among the best-selling lines. . . . No doubt

the ghoulish traffic in the verse exercises of dead schoolboys was an excellent business proposition . . .

Douglas Goldring, from Reputations

The grandly vague style of these poems was made fun of by a famous critic: 'They turn out their works on a formula. Put England down as "knightly", state her honour to be "inviolate" . . . introduce a "thou" or two, and conclude with the assertion that God will defend the Right – and there's the formula for a poem.'

A third wave of war poetry – by Wilfred Owen, Siegfried Sassoon and others – is that which is now remembered and admired. Owen resented the fake 'heroes' who were invented in the early war verse. He wanted to tell the truth about the real heroism and suffering that he had seen in France. Sassoon also wished to tell the public about the Western Front, the 'hell where youth and laughter go'. He spoke up for the courage and endurance of

The unreturning army that was youth;
The legions who have suffered and are dust.

from Prelude: The Troops

UNIT 8 *Recruiting poems*

When war began in August 1914, Britain, unlike other European powers which had huge conscript armies, relied only on a small professional force. Lord Kitchener, Secretary of State for War, saw that the conflict would be long and hard fought, and proposed a revolutionary plan for 'New Armies' of millions of volunteers. His own grim face, over the slogan 'Your King and Country Need You', appeared in the first poster appeal for recruits. Until conscription was introduced in 1916, young men were subjected to relentless social pressures, both official and unofficial, to join the army.

Newspapers of all kinds gave space to recruiting poems. Harold Begbie's *Fall In*, which first appeared in the *Daily Chronicle* on 31 August 1914, became tremendously popular. It was set to music and sung in music halls; posters and badges related to the poem were produced: 'Sing the Song! Wear the Badge! Play the March!'

Fall In

What will you lack, sonny, what will you lack
  When the girls line up the street,
Shouting their love to the lads come back
  From the foe they rushed to beat?
Will you send a strangled cheer to the sky
  And grin till your cheeks are red?
But what will you lack when your mate goes by
  With a girl who cuts you dead?[1]

Where will you look, sonny, where will you look
  When your children yet to be
Clamour to learn of the part you took
  In the War that kept men free?
Will you say it was naught to you if France
  Stood up to her foe or bunked?
But where will you look when they give you the glance
  That tells you they know you funked?

How will you fare, sonny, how will you fare
  In the far-off winter night,
When you sit by the fire in an old man's chair
  And your neighbours talk of the fight?
Will you slink away, as it were from a blow,
  Your old head shamed and bent?
Or say – I was not with the first to go,
  But I went, thank God, I went?

Why do they call, sonny, why do they call
  For men who are brave and strong?
Is it naught to you if your country fall,
  And Right is smashed by Wrong?
Is it football still and the picture show,
  The pub and the betting odds,
When your brothers stand to the tyrant's blow
  And Britain's call is God's?

HAROLD BEGBIE

[1] ignores you

Begbie tries to make 'shirkers' feel ashamed of not volunteering. What methods does he use to create shame?
Suppose that you could argue with Begbie. What answers would you give to his points?

Matilda Betham-Edwards was a popular Victorian writer who had worked, in her youth, with Charles Dickens. Now aged 78, she 'did her bit' for the war effort with this poem.

The Two Mothers

'Poor woman, weeping as they pass,
  Yon brave recruits, the nation's pride,
You mourn some gallant boy, alas!
  Like mine who lately fought and died?'

'Kind stranger, not for soldier son,
  Of shame, not grief, my heart will break,
Three stalwarts have I, but not one
  Doth risk his life for England's sake!'

MATILDA BETHAM-EDWARDS

At whom is this poem aimed?
What is the point of this conversation between mothers?
How is the poem like this recruiting poster?

Jessie Pope composed crude war verses for the *Daily Mail*. She was particularly detested by the great soldier poet Wilfred Owen, who saw her as typical of the unfeeling civilian who was supporting the war from the relative safety of the Home Front.

Who's for the Game?

Who's for the game, the biggest that's played,
    The red crashing game of a fight?
Who'll grip and tackle the job unafraid?
    And who thinks he'd rather sit tight?

Who'll toe the line for the signal to 'Go!'?
    Who'll give his country a hand?
Who wants a turn to himself in the show?
    And who wants a seat in the stand?

Who knows it won't be a picnic – not much –
    Yet eagerly shoulders a gun?
Who would much rather come back with a crutch
    Than lie low and be out of the fun?

Come along, lads – but you'll come on all right –
    For there's only one course to pursue,
Your country is up to her neck in a fight,
    And she's looking and calling for you.

                    JESSIE POPE

Why does Jessie Pope use this slang style ('sit tight', 'up to her neck', etc.)?
The poet uses a comparison throughout this poem. What is it? What is your opinion of it?
What do you think of the poet's phrases:
    rather come back with a crutch
    out of the fun . . .?

E.A.Mackintosh left Oxford University to volunteer. He was a gallant soldier, who won the Military Cross, and was gassed and wounded at the Battle of the Somme. He was killed at Cambrai in 1917. His battle experience made him cynical about recruiting posters and their slogans.

Recruiting

'Lads, you're wanted, go and help,'
On the railway carriage wall
Stuck the poster, and I thought
Of the hands that penned the call.

Fat civilians wishing they
'Could go and fight the Hun'.
Can't you see them thanking God
That they're over forty-one?

Girls with feathers,[1] vulgar songs –
Washy verse on England's need –

God – and don't we damned well know
How the message ought to read.

'Lads, you're wanted! over there,
Shiver in the morning dew,
More poor devils like yourselves
Waiting to be killed by you.

Go and help to swell the names
In the casualty lists.
Help to make the column's stuff
For the blasted journalists.

Help to keep them nice and safe
From the wicked German foe.
Don't let him come over here!
Lads, you're wanted – out you go.'

There's a better word than that,
Lads, and can't you hear it come
From a million men that call
You to share their martyrdom?

Leave the harlots still to sing
Comic songs about the Hun,
Leave the fat old men to say
Now *we've* got them on the run.

Better twenty honest years
Than their dull three score and ten.
Lads, you're wanted. Come and learn
To live and die with honest men.

You shall learn what men can do
If you will but pay the price,
Learn the gaiety and strength
In the gallant sacrifice.

Take your risk of life and death
Underneath the open sky.
Live clean or go out quick –
Lads, you're wanted. Come and die.

> E.A. MACKINTOSH

[1] some women gave white feathers to 'cowards' who were not in uniform

The poet sees a recruiting poster. It makes him think of aspects of life in war-time Britain that he detests. What are these?
Who are the 'poor devils' in the fourth verse?
Why are they 'shivering in the morning dew'?
The words 'over there' make the poet reflect that he intensely admires and respects certain things about the soldiers in France and Flanders. What are these things?

W Write about the poems in this section.
What is each poem about?
What methods do the writers use to win over the reader?
What do you like or dislike about the poems?

W Write your own recruiting poem in the style of the 1914 writers.
You have to make war sound glamorous, exciting and manly.

W This young man *has* volunteered for the army and is about to leave for war service abroad. Imagine the thoughts of each of the people in the picture, perhaps a mixture of pride, excitement and sadness. Write a paragraph about each person; then add another expressing your own thoughts, or imagining the fate of the soldier.

W Write a short story based on this photograph.

A soldier's goodbye photographed by F.J. Mortimer, 1914

D Look carefully at the 1914-18 recruiting posters opposite. Discuss them in pairs.
What is the message of each poster?
How do they attempt to persuade men to join the army?
Which is most effective?

W Draw your own recruiting poster and invent a good slogan, or devise an anti-war poster and slogan. Write a short persuasive speech to match your poster.

Recruiting posters

In May 1915, the British liner Lusitania was sunk by a German
U-boat off the Irish coast and 2000 people, including many women
and children, were drowned

Daddy, what did **YOU** do in the Great War?

ENLIST

Are **YOU** in this?

UNIT 9   *Ideals and chivalry*

In 1914, most British people had forgotten what war was actually like. There had not been a major European conflict for a century. Only professional soldiers had fought in South Africa. Young men were restless. To us, the Edwardian era may seem glamorous but to people of the time it was stuffy and dull, and also shameful with its strikes, suffragette riots, and its extremes of wealth and poverty. In August 1914, the war seemed a glorious adventure.

Poets reflected this enthusiasm. They showed the war as an epic. Honour, Glory, Sacrifice were key words. Ideals of chivalry, the old code of medieval knights, were taken from Victorian writers and painters who had loved the stories of King Arthur. A soldier was now a 'warrior'; the enemy the 'foe'. The dead were the 'fallen'; fighting was 'strife'. 'Guerdon', a knight's reward for service, was often used. Here is a selection of such poems, some of them much admired in their day.

The Volunteer

Here lies a clerk who half his life had spent
Toiling at ledgers in a city grey,
Thinking that so his days would drift away
With no lance broken in life's tournament.
Yet ever 'twixt the books and his bright eyes
The gleaming eagles of the legions came,
And horsemen, charging under phantom skies,
Went thundering past beneath the oriflamme.[1]

And now those waiting dreams are satisfied;
From twilight to the halls of dawn he went;
His lance is broken; but he lies content
With that high hour, in which he lived and died.
And falling thus he wants no recompense,
Who found his battle in the last resort;
Nor need he any hearse to bear him hence,
Who goes to join the men of Agincourt.[2]

HERBERT ASQUITH

[1] banner
[2] Henry V's victory in France, 1415

What was the clerk's pre-war life like? What did he dream about at his desk?

What happened to him in the war? What did he feel as he died?
How does Asquith feel about the clerk's fate?
Do you like the ideals of this poem/the old-fashioned words?

Rupert Brooke was the most famous poet of the first part of the war. His sonnets (poems of 14 lines and a set verse pattern) caused a sensation when they appeared just after his death on the way to Gallipoli in 1915.

Peace

Now, God be thanked Who has matched us with His
     hour,
And caught our youth, and wakened us from sleeping,
With hand made sure, clear eye, and sharpened power,
To turn, as swimmers into cleanness leaping,
Glad from a world grown old and cold and weary,
Leave the sick hearts that honour could not move,
And half-men, and their dirty songs and dreary,
And all the little emptiness of love!

Oh! we, who have known shame, we have found
     release there,
Where there's no ill, no grief, but sleep has mending,
Naught broken save this body, lost but breath;
Nothing to shake the laughing heart's long peace there
But only agony, and that has ending;
And the worst friend and enemy is but Death.

RUPERT BROOKE

Does Brooke see his generation as lucky or unlucky?
What has the war done to young men?
Explain the comparisons about the sleepers and the swimmers. Do you like these?
What does Brooke despise about the pre-war world?
Most people would fear death or wounds in war. What does Brooke say about them in the second part of the poem?
Why is the poem called *Peace*?

The popular Irish poet Katherine Tynan worked as a nurse, while her two sons fought at the front. She thought that the war was necessary and just, and a good thing for young men.

To the Others

This was the gleam then that lured from far
Your son and my son to the Holy War:
Your son and my son for the accolade
With the banner of Christ over them, in steel arrayed.

All quiet roads of life ran on to this
When they were little for their mother's kiss;
Little feet hastening, so soft, unworn,
To the vows and the vigil and the road of thorn.

Your son and my son, the downy things,
Sheltered in mother's breast, by mother's wings;
Should they be broken in the Lord's wars – Peace!
He who has given them are they not His?

Dreams of knight's armour and the battle shout,
Fighting and falling at the last redoubt;[1]
Dreams of long dying on the field of slain:
This was the dream that lured, nor lured in vain.

These were the Voices they heard from far,
Bugles and trumpets of the Holy War;
Your son and my son have heard the call,
Your son and my son have stormed the wall.

Your son and my son, clean as new swords,
Your man and my man and now the Lord's!
Your son and my son for the Great Crusade,
With the banner of Christ over them – our knights, new
  made.

KATHERINE TYNAN

[1] fort

What are the soldiers compared to throughout the poem? Which words and phrases support this idea?
Which words tell you that the poet thinks the war is worthwhile?
How does she console mothers who may lose their sons?
Do you like this poem?

John McCrae was a Canadian doctor who wrote this poem at a dressing-station for the wounded near Ypres in 1915. His poem saw a link between the dead and the poppies that grew on their graves. After the war, this gave rise to the poppy symbol that is still used on Remembrance Day. McCrae himself died in 1918.

In Flanders Fields

In Flanders fields the poppies blow
Between the crosses, row on row
   That mark our place; and in the sky
   The larks, still bravely singing, fly
Scarce heard amid the guns below.

We are the Dead. Short days ago
We lived, felt dawn, saw sunset glow,
   Loved and were loved, and now we lie
      In Flanders fields.

Take up our quarrel with the foe:
To you from failing hands we throw
   The torch; be yours to hold it high.
   If ye break faith with us who die
We shall not sleep, though poppies grow
      In Flanders fields.

JOHN McCRAE

How does the poet contrast life and death in the first two verses?
The dead speak. How do they remember life?
What is their message to other living soldiers?

Laurence Binyon's *For the Fallen* is also widely quoted on Remembrance Day. Aged 45 when the war began, he served as a Red Cross orderly in France and was deeply moved by the destruction of the younger generation. Here are the last two verses:

from: For the Fallen

They went with songs to the battle, they were young,
Straight of limb, true of eye, steady and aglow.
They were staunch to the end against odds uncounted:
They fell with their faces to the foe.

They shall grow not old, as we that are left grow old:
Age shall not weary them, nor the years condemn.
At the going down of the sun and in the morning
We will remember them.

LAURENCE BINYON

What good qualities does he see in the young soldiers?
What does 'faces to the foe' mean?
How do they remain in the minds of the survivors?
What, by contrast, happens to the survivors?
Do you like the old-fashioned words? Why does Binyon use them?
The poem is so familiar that it is hard to see it freshly. What do you think of these verses of *For the Fallen* **and their message?**

Robert Nichols was shell-shocked at the Somme in 1916. This is a sketch of the ruined battlefield.

Dawn on the Somme

Last night rain fell over the scarred plateau,
And now from the dark horizon, dazzling, flies
Arrow on fire-plumed arrow to the skies,
Shot from the bright arc of Apollo's[1] bow;
And from the wild and writhen[2] waste below,
From flashing pools and mounds lit one by one,
Oh, is it mist, or are these companies
Of morning heroes who arise, arise
With thrusting arms, with limbs and hair aglow,
Toward the risen god, upon whose brow
Burns the gold laurel of all victories,
Hero and heroes' god, th' invincible Sun?

ROBERT NICHOLS

[1] ancient Greek idea that the sun was a god
[2] smashed and twisted

Sunrise makes the morning mists rise. What comparisons does this create in the poet's mind? Do you find these comparisons moving or artificial?

W Write about some or all of this group of poems, saying how the poets see:
   soldiers in battle,
   death in war,
   war itself.

Consider some of the comparisons and old-fashioned words that are used by the poets. Give your opinions of the poems: what do you like or dislike about them?

D Tale of a glorious end
This drawing appeared in the *Illustrated London News* of Christmas 1914. It shows war as people wanted to see it: as noble, heroic sacrifice. Discuss the details of the picture: the sword on the table; the portrait; the friend's slight wound; the old man's pose; the young wife's expression; the grey-haired mother.

Tale of a glorious end

D Dead German in a trench
This photograph was taken at Beaumont-Hamel on the Somme after the battle there in November 1916. Contrast its horrible details with the *Tale of a glorious end*.

German corpse, Beaumont-Hamel, the Somme, November 1916

UNIT 10   *Realities of trench warfare*

Men who had to fight the nightmare battles of the Western Front felt that the picture of war as a knightly adventure was false and stupid. A new, plain, blunt style of poem showed the horrors forcefully. Old-fashioned epic language gave way to soldiers' slang.

Robert Graves fought at Mametz Wood on the Somme in July 1916 and could never forget the casualties he saw there. ('Boche' was French soldiers' slang for a German.)

A Dead Boche

To you who'd read my songs of War
    And only hear of blood and fame,
I'll say (you've heard it said before)
    'War's Hell!' and if you doubt the same,
Today I found in Mametz Wood
A certain cure for lust of blood:

Where, propped against a shattered trunk,
    In a great mess of things unclean,
Sat a dead Boche; he scowled and stunk
    With clothes and face a sodden green,
Big-bellied, spectacled, crop-haired,
Dribbling black blood from nose and beard.

ROBERT GRAVES

What is 'lust of blood'?
What is so horrible about the dead German?
Why is he a 'certain cure'? What is Graves'
message here?
Do you like the plain language of the poem?

Ruth Comfort Mitchell was an American poet,
who imagined the effects of war in Europe. She
tells the story of an ordinary young volunteer.

He went for a Soldier

He marched away with a blithe young score of him
  With the first volunteers,
Clear-eyed and clean and sound to the core of him,
  Blushing under the cheers.
They were fine, new flags that swung a-flying there,
Oh, the pretty girls he glimpsed a-crying there,
  Pelting him with pinks and roses –
  Billy, the Soldier Boy!

Not very clear in the kind young heart of him
  What the fuss was about,
But the flowers and the flags seemed part of him –
  The music drowned his doubt.
It's a fine, brave sight they were a-coming there
To the gay, bold tune they kept a-drumming there,
  While the boasting fifes shrilled jauntily –
  Billy, the Soldier Boy!

Soon he is one with the blinding smoke of it –
  Volley and curse and groan:
Then he has done with the knightly joke of it –
  It's rending flesh and bone.
There are pain-crazed animals a-shrieking there
And a warm blood stench that is a-reeking there;
  He fights like a rat in a corner –
  Billy, the Soldier Boy!

There he lies now, like a ghoulish score of him,
  Left on the field for dead:
The ground all around is smeared with the gore of him –
  Even the leaves are red.
The Thing that was Billy lies a-dying there,
Writhing and a-twisting and a-crying there;
  A sickening sun grins down on him –
  Billy, the Soldier Boy!

Still not quite clear in the poor, wrung heart of him
  What the fuss was about,
See where he lies – or a ghastly part of him –
  While life is oozing out:
There are loathsome things he sees a-crawling there;
There are hoarse-voiced crows he hears a-calling there,
  Eager for the foul feast spread for them –
  Billy, the Soldier Boy!

RUTH COMFORT MITCHELL

What sort of a boy is Billy?
Why does war seem exciting at first? What
doesn't he understand about it?
What does 'knightly joke' mean?
Which words and comparisons describe the
horror of battle? Which do you find most
vivid?
What various contrasts does this poem show
us about war?

W Write a story based on the experiences of
Billy. You will need some extra introduction:
his family; where he lived; how he
volunteered. Base the rest of his experiences
closely on the poem.

Arthur Graeme West wrote some good poetry and
an interesting diary before he was killed in 1917. In
this extract from a poem, he attacks the attitudes of
a soldier poet, Hugh Freston, who wrote a heroic-
style sonnet beginning

Oh happy to have lived these epic days!
  To have seen unfold, as doth a dream unfold,
These glorious chivalries, these deeds of gold . . .

West uses horrific details of trench fighting to
answer him.

God! How I hate you

God! how I hate you, you young cheerful men,
Whose pious poetry blossoms on your graves
As soon as you are in them . . .
                              Hark how one chants –
'Oh happy to have lived these epic days' –
'These epic days'! And *he'd* been to France,
And seen the trenches, glimpsed the huddled dead
In the periscope, hung on the rusty wire:
Choked by their sickly foetor,[1] day and night
Blown down his throat: stumbled through ruined
  hearths,
Proved all that muddy brown monotony
Where blood's the only coloured thing. Perhaps
Had seen a man killed, a sentry shot at night,
Hunched as he fell, his feet on the firing-step,
His neck against the back slope of the trench,
And the rest doubled between, his head
Smashed like an eggshell and the warm grey brain
Spattered all bloody on the parados[2] . . .
Yet still God's in His Heaven, all is right
In this best possible of worlds . . .

ARTHUR GRAEME WEST

[1] stink
[2] rear sandbag parapet of trench

Which details do you find most impressive? Do you like the blunt language and the sarcastic last line?

Gilbert Frankau also attacked the heroic-style war poets. He had read the poems of a fellow officer who had been promoted to the Staff and so had escaped the trenches. He wrote him a verse letter, called *The Other Side*, from which these are extracts.

from: *The Other Side*

About your book. I've read it carefully,
So has Macfaddyen; (you remember him,
The light-haired chap who joined us after Loos?);[1]
And candidly, we don't think much of it.
The piece about the horses isn't bad;
But all the rest, excuse the word, are tripe –
The same old tripe we've read a thousand times.

My grief, but we're fed up to the back teeth
With war-books, war-verse, all the eye-wash stuff
That seems to please the idiots at home.
You know the kind of thing, or used to know:
'Heroes who laugh while Fritz is strafing them' –
(I don't remember that *you* found it fun,
The day they shelled us out of Blauwport Farm!)
'After the fight. Our cheery wounded. Note
The smile of victory: it won't come off' –
(Of course they smile; so'd you, if you'd escaped,
And saw three months of hospital ahead . . .
They don't smile, much, when they're shipped
  back to France!)
But what's the good of war-books, if they fail
To give civilian-readers an idea
Of what life *is* like in the firing line. . . .

You might have done that much; from you, at least,
I thought we'd get an inkling of the truth.
But no; you rant and rattle, beat your drum,
And blow your two-penny trumpet like the rest:
'Red battle's glory,' 'Honour's utmost task,'
'Gay jesting faces of undaunted boys,' . . .
The same old Boy's-Own-Paper balderdash! . . .

Hang it, you can't have clean forgotten things
You went to bed with, woke with, smelt and felt,
All those long months of boredom streaked with fear:
Mud, cold, fatigue, sweat, nerve-strain, sleeplessness,
And men's excreta viscid in the rain,
And stiff-legged horses lying by the road,
Their bloated bellies shimmering, green with flies . . .

You *have* forgotten; or you couldn't write
This sort of stuff – all cant, no guts in it,
Hardly a single picture true to life.

Well, here's a picture for you: Montauban[2] –
Last year – the flattened village on our left –
On our right flank, the razed Briqueterie,
Their five-nines pounding bits to dustier bits –
Behind, a cratered slope, with batteries
Crashing and flashing, violet in the dusk,
And prematuring every now and then –
In front, the ragged Bois de Bernafay,
Boche whizz-bangs bursting white among its trees.
You had been doing F.O.O.[3] that day;
(The Staff knows why we had an F.O.O.:
One couldn't flag-wag through Trônes Wood; the wires
Went down as fast as one could put them up;
And messages by runner took three hours.)
I'd got the wind up rather: you were late,
And they'd been shelling like the very deuce.
However, back you came. I see you now,
Staggering into 'mess' – a broken trench,
Two chalk-walls roofed with corrugated iron,
And, round the traverse, Driver Noakes's stove
Stinking and smoking while we ate our grub.
Your face was blue-white, streaked with dirt; your eyes
Had shrunk into your head, as though afraid
To watch more horrors; you were sodden-wet
With greasy coal-black mud – and other things.
Sweating and shivering, speechless, there you stood.
I gave you whisky, made you talk. You said:
'Major, another signaller's been killed.'
'Who?'
          'Gunner Andrews, blast them. O my Christ!
His head – split open – when his brains oozed out,
They looked like bloody sweetbreads, in the muck.'

And you're the chap who writes this clap-trap verse!

Lord, if I'd half *your* brains, I'd write a book:
None of your sentimental platitudes,
But something real, vital; that should strip
The glamour from this outrage we call war,
Showing it naked, hideous, stupid, vile –
One vast abomination. So that they
Who, coming after, till the ransomed fields
Where our lean corpses rotted in the ooze,
Reading my written words, should understand
This stark stupendous horror, visualise
The unutterable foulness of it all. . . .
I'd show them, not your glamorous 'glorious game,'
Which men play 'jesting' 'for their honour's sake' –
(A kind of Military Tournament,
With just a hint of danger – bound in cloth!) –
But War, – as war is now, and always was:
A dirty, loathsome, servile murder-job: –
Men, lousy, sleepless, ulcerous, afraid,
Toiling their hearts out in the pulling slime
That wrenches gum-boots down from bleeding heel
And cakes in itching arm-pits, navel, ears:
Men stunned to brainlessness, and gibbering:
Men driving men to death, and worse than death:
Men maimed and blinded: men against machines –

Flesh versus iron, concrete, flame and wire:
Men choking out their souls in poison-gas:
Men squelched into the slime by trampling feet:
Men, disembowelled by guns five miles away,
Cursing, with their last breath, the living God
Because He made them, in His image, men. . . .
So – were your talent mine – I'd write of war
For those who, coming after, know it not. . . .

                                    GILBERT FRANKAU

[1] battle, 1915
[2] on the Somme, 1916
[3] Forward Observation Officer

Frankau uses soldiers' slang as part of his
effect here. Find some examples. Then find
some words and phrases from typical 'heroic'
war poets and newspapermen.
How does Frankau use exact, horrible details
in his Somme story?
What does he want to do to the reader?
What is the purpose of the long list of war's
horrors at the end of the extract?
What does Frankau want to do in this poem?

W Write your own letter to the friend, using
ideas and style from Frankau's poem.

In *Counter-Attack*, Siegfried Sassoon describes how
British troops capture a German trench system. As
dawn comes, they realize the horror of their
surroundings. This is an extract.

from: *Counter-Attack*

We'd gained our first objective hours before
While dawn broke like a face with blinking eyes,
Pallid, unshaved and thirsty, blind with smoke.
Things seemed all right at first. We held their line,
With bombers posted, Lewis guns well placed,
And clink of shovels deepening the shallow trench.
The place was rotten with dead; green clumsy legs
High-booted, sprawled and grovelled along the saps
And trunks, face downward, in the sucking mud,
Wallowed like trodden sand-bags loosely filled;
And naked sodden buttocks, mats of hair,
Bulged, clotted heads slept in the plastering slime.
And then the rain began, – the jolly old rain!

                                    SIEGFRIED SASSOON

What is the dawn compared to?
Why is this especially suitable?

What do the men discover as daylight comes?
Sassoon uses words that are not only about
ugly ideas but are also ugly to *say*. Pick out
some of these.
What is Sassoon's intention in this extract?

W Look back over the poems and extracts in this
section. Write about some or all of the poems.
Say how they use:
    realistic pictures of trench incidents,
    horrible details,
    plain conversational English,
    vivid comparisons.
Which do you find most impressive?

W Compare some of the poems of 'ideals' to
some of the poems of 'reality'. Mention:
    attitudes to war,
    vague generalities/particular details,
    language/comparisons used.

The horrors of the Western Front: from the series
Der Krieg (The War) by the German artist, Otto Dix

Trench suicide

Bringing up supplies

Dead men in a trench

UNIT 11   *Comrades: a verse short story*

Comrades: an Episode, by Robert Nichols, is a story about the close relationship between an officer and his men. When Gates, the officer, is hit and badly wounded, he manages to crawl back across No Man's Land to his own parapet; there two of his men sacrifice their lives to help him.

In a world where life seemed pointless and death always near, only comradeship remained as a worthwhile purpose. 'It was just a human relationship,' said the soldier–writer Richard Aldington, 'an undemonstrative exchange of sympathies between ordinary men racked to extremity under a great common strain in a great common danger.' To support and be faithful to your comrades: that was the bond which held together the morale of the armies.

Comrades: An Episode

Before, before he was aware
The 'Verey' light[1] had risen . . . on the air
It hung glistering . . .
        And he could not stay his hand
From moving to the barbed wire's broken strand.
A rifle cracked.
     He fell.
Night waned. He was alone. A heavy shell
Whispered itself passing high, high overhead.
His wound was wet to his hand: for still it bled
On to the glimmering ground.
Then with a slow, vain smile his wound he bound,
Knowing, of course, he'd not see home again –
Home whose thought he put away.
         His men
Whispered: 'Where's Mister Gates?' 'Out on the wire.'
'I'll get him,' said one . . .
        Dawn blinked, and the fire
Of the Germans heaved up and down the line.
'Stand to'[2]
      Too late! 'I'll get him.' 'O the swine!
When we might get him in yet safe and whole!'
'Corporal didn't see 'un fall out on patrol.
Or he'd 'a got 'un.' 'Sssh!'
        'No talking there.'
A whisper: ' 'A went down at the last flare.'
Meanwhile the Maxims[3] toc-toc-tocked; their swish
Of bullets told death lurked against the wish.
No hope for him!
      His corporal, as one shamed,
Vainly and helplessly his ill-luck blamed.

Then Gates slowly saw the morn
Break in a rosy peace through the lone thorn
By which he lay, and felt the dawn-wind pass
Whispering through the pallid, stalky grass
Of No-Man's Land . . .
          And the tears came
Scaldingly sweet, more lovely than a flame.
He closed his eyes: he thought of home
And grit his teeth. He knew no help could come . . .

The silent sun over the earth held sway,
Occasional rifles cracked and far away
A heedless speck, a 'plane, slid on alone,
Like a fly traversing a cliff of stone.
'I must get back', said Gates aloud, and heaved
At his body. But it lay bereaved
Of any power. He could not wait till night . . .
And he lay still. Blood swam across his sight.
Then with a groan:
'No luck ever! Well, I must die alone'.

Occasional rifles cracked. A cloud that shone,
Gold-rimmed, blackened the sun and then was
   gone . . .
The sun still smiled. The grass sang in its play.
Someone whistled: 'Over the hills and far away'.
Gates watched silently the swift, swift sun
Burning his life before it was begun . . .

Suddenly he heard Corporal Timmins' voice: 'Now
  then,
'Urry up with that tea.'
         'Hi Ginger!' 'Bill!' His men!
Timmins and Jones and Wilkinson (the 'bard'),
And Hughes and Simpson. It was hard
Not to see them: Wilkinson, stubby, grim,
With his 'No, sir,' 'Yes, sir,' and the slim
Simpson: 'Indeed, sir?' (while it seemed he winked
Because his smiling left eye always blinked)
And Corporal Timmins, straight and blond and wise,
With his quiet-scanning, level, hazel eyes;
And all the others . . . tunics that didn't fit . . .
A dozen different sorts of eyes. O it
Was hard to lie there! Yet he must. But no:
'I've got to die. I'll get to them. I'll go'.

Inch by inch he fought, breathless and mute,
Dragging his carcase like a famished brute . . .
His head was hammering, and his eyes were dim;
A bloody sweat seemed to ooze out of him
And freeze along his spine . . . Then he'd lie still
Before another effort of his will

Took him one nearer yard.
                    The parapet was reached.
He could not rise to it. A lookout screeched:
'Mr Gates!'
              Three figures in one breath
Leaped up. Two figures fell in toppling death;
And Gates was lifted in. 'Who's hit?' said he.
'Timmins and Jones.' 'Why did they that for me? –
I'm gone already!' Gently they laid him prone
And silently watched.
                    He twitched. They heard him moan

'Why for me?' His eyes roamed round, and none
    replied.
'I see it was alone I should have died.'
They shook their heads. Then, 'Is the doctor here?'
'He's coming, sir, he's hurryin', no fear.'
'No good . . .
              Lift me.' They lifted him.
He smiled and held his arms out to the dim,
And in a moment passed beyond their ken,
Hearing him whisper, 'O my men, my men!'

                              ROBERT NICHOLS

[1] flare to light up trench area
[2] trench alert at dawn
[3] machine-guns

W **When you have read the poem carefully, write a story based closely on the events and characters that it contains. Try to make its theme of comradeship stand out. You will need to add some material from your own imagination. You may find this photograph of British troops, on the Somme in July 1916, useful in rounding out the characters in your story.**

British troops in the trenches at the Somme, July 1916

UNIT 12   *Spring offensive*

Each year of the First World War was marked by massive spring attacks by one side or the other. All were unsuccessful until the Germans finally smashed the Western Front in March 1918. Many writers noted the contrast between the new life and energy of spring, and the death and destruction of battle.

A little group of men with scarlet staff-bands on their caps and tabs on their collars climb out of the cars and prod sticks at the ground, stamp on it, dig a heel in, to test its hardness and dryness. . . . To these men the 'Promise of Spring' is the promise of the crescendo of battle and slaughter.

The General and his staff are standing in the middle of a wide patch of poppies, spread out in a bright scarlet that matches exactly the red splashes on the brows and throats of the group. They move slowly back towards the cars, and as they walk the red ripples and swirls against their boots and about their knees.

One might imagine them wading knee deep in a river of blood . . .

Boyd Cable, from *Between the Lines*

Wilfred Owen's last poem is based on this contrast. He had taken part in an attack in May 1917, which he described in a letter.

The sensations of going over the top are about as exhilarating as those dreams of falling over a precipice. . . . There was an extraordinary exultation in the act of slowly walking forward, showing ourselves openly. . . . When I looked back and saw the ground all crawling and wormy with wounded bodies, I felt no horror at all but only an immense exultation at having got through the barrage . . .

Wilfred Owen, 17 May 1917

He used some of those ideas in the poem.

Spring Offensive

Halted against the shade of a last hill
They fed, and eased of pack-loads, were at ease;
And leaning on the nearest chest or knees
Carelessly slept.
                              But many there stood still
To face the stark blank sky beyond the ridge,
Knowing their feet had come to the end of the world.
Marvelling they stood, and watched the long grass
    swirled
By the May breeze, murmurous with wasp and midge;
And though the summer oozed into their veins
Like an injected drug for their bodies' pains,
Sharp on their souls hung the imminent ridge of grass,
Fearfully flashed the sky's mysterious glass.

Hour after hour they ponder the warm field
And the far valley behind, where buttercups
Had blessed with gold their slow boots coming up;
When even the little brambles would not yield
But clutched and clung to them like sorrowing arms.
They breathe like trees unstirred.

Till like a cold gust thrills the little word
At which each body and its soul begird[1]
And tighten them for battle. No alarms
Of bugles, no high flags, no clamorous haste, –
Only a lift and flare of eyes that faced
The sun, like a friend with whom their love is done.
O larger shone that smile against the sun, –
Mightier than his whose bounty these have spurned.

So, soon they topped the hill, and raced together
Over an open stretch of herb and heather
Exposed. And instantly the whole sky burned
With fury against them; earth set sudden cups[2]
In thousands for their blood; and the green slope
Chasmed and deepened sheer to infinite space.

Of them who running on that last high place
Breasted the surf of bullets, or went up
On the hot blast and fury of hell's upsurge,
Or plunged and fell away past this world's verge,
Some say God caught them even before they fell.

But what say such as from existence' brink
Ventured but drave[3] too swift to sink,
The few who rushed in the body to enter hell,
And there out-fiending all its fiends and flames
With superhuman inhumanities,
Long-famous glories, immemorial shames –
And crawling slowly back, have by degrees
Regained cool peaceful air in wonder –
Why speak not they of comrades that went under?

WILFRED OWEN

[1] get ready
[2] literally: shell holes
[3] drove

What are the soldiers doing in the first three verses?
What is 'beyond the ridge'?
Why have their feet come 'to the end of the world'?
Look at the lines 'Marvelling they stood . . . bodies' pains'. Owen uses the *sound* of words to create a mood. What mood? Which words?

What does nature seem to be doing to the soldiers in the third verse?
How do the men feel about the spring world and life itself before the battle?
What is the 'little word'?
What do the men look at last as they say goodbye to the world? Why?
What do they not care about at that time?

The last three verses describe the attack. What happens when they cross the hill top? 'Sudden cups' are shell holes but the word also suggests some Druid ceremony where old men caught the blood of young victims in sacred cups. Do you find this idea impressive? Owen uses short, blunt words to suggest the violence of battle. Pick out some of these. Why, for some, does the green slope turn into infinite space?
Do you think that Owen believes in the after-life? Which words contain his doubt? Some men survive. At what do they first look? What do they *not* talk about? Do you find this strange?

W Imagine that you are one of the soldiers who survived. Keeping close to the ideas of the poem, describe your thoughts and observations before, during and after the battle.

Julian Grenfell's *Into Battle* was, in its time, one of the most popular poems produced by the war. It was published in *The Times* in May 1915, shortly after Grenfell died from wounds. Whatever his private thoughts, in his letters home he put on an appearance of enjoying the fighting. 'I adore war. . . . It is like a big picnic. . . . It's all the best fun one ever dreamed of.' *Into Battle* is written in this spirit. Grenfell's picture of the soldier in spring contrasts strongly with Owen's.

Into Battle

The naked earth is warm with spring,
    And with green grass and bursting trees
Leans to the sun's gaze glorying,
    And quivers in the sunny breeze;

And life is colour and warmth and light,
    And a striving evermore for these;
And he is dead who will not fight;
    And who dies fighting has increase.

The fighting man shall from the sun
    Take warmth, and life from the glowing earth;
Speed with the light-foot winds to run,
    And with the trees to newer birth;
And find, when fighting shall be done,
    Great rest, and fullness after dearth.

All the bright company of Heaven
    Hold him in their high comradeship,
The Dog-Star, and the Sisters Seven,
    Orion's Belt and sworded hip.

The woodland trees that stand together,
    They stand to him each one a friend;
They gently speak in the windy weather:
    They guide to valley and ridge's end.

The kestrel hovering by day,
    And the little owls that call by night,
Bid him be swift and keen as they,
    As keen of ear, as swift of sight.

The blackbird sings to him, 'Brother, brother,
    If this be the last song you shall sing,
Sing well, for you may not sing another;
    Brother, sing.'

In dreary, doubtful, waiting hours,
    Before the brazen frenzy starts,
The horses show him nobler powers;
    O patient eyes, courageous hearts!

And when the burning moment breaks,
    And all things else are out of mind,
And only joy of battle takes
    Him by the throat, and makes him blind,

Through joy and blindness he shall know,
    Not caring much to know, that still
Nor lead nor steel shall reach him, so
    That it be not the Destined Will.

The thundering line of battle stands,
    And in the air Death moans and sings;
But Day shall clasp him with strong hands,
    And Night shall fold him in soft wings.

JULIAN GRENFELL

What impression of spring is given in the first two verses? Which words create this?
Life seems to be a struggle to survive. How does the soldier therefore seem to be a part of nature?
Which parts of the natural world seem to support the soldier?
How does Grenfell try to calm the soldier's fears before the attack?
This is a poem full of bold words and ideas that make it good to recite. Which lines are your favourites?

W Compare *Spring Offensive* and *Into Battle*.
How do both poets use spring as the background to battle?
How do they feel about fighting and about life?
How do they describe the experience of battle?
What are their attitudes to death in war?
Compare the language of the two poems. Which do you find more attractive and convincing? Which do you prefer and why?

UNIT 13   *Winter war*

'Winter is not the least of the horrors of war,' wrote the soldier poet Isaac Rosenberg in a letter. As a private he had to endure the hardships of the Western Front for months on end. The old idea of armies ceasing fire in autumn to retire into winter quarters had vanished by 1914. Trench fighting continued throughout the winters of the First World War. Even the famous Christmas truces, when enemies mingled cheerfully in No Man's Land, ended after 1915.

Wilfred Owen first went to the Front in the Somme sector in the bitter winter of 1916-17. In January, he wrote to his mother, describing the bleak landscape.

No Man's Land under snow is like the face of the moon: chaotic, crater-ridden, uninhabitable, awful, the abode of madness. . . . My platoon had no dug-outs, but had to lie out in the snow under the deadly wind. . . .

We were marooned on a frozen desert. There was not a sign of life on the horizon and a thousand signs of death. Not a blade of grass. Not an insect: once or twice a day the shadow of a big hawk scenting carrion . . .

Wilfred Owen, January 1917

His poem *Exposure* came out of this experience.

Exposure

Our brains ache, in the merciless iced east winds that
    knive us . . .
Wearied we keep awake because the night is silent . . .
Low, drooping flares confuse our memory of the
    salient[1] . . .
Worried by silence, sentries whisper, curious, nervous,
        But nothing happens.

Watching, we hear the mad gusts tugging on the wire,
Like twitching agonies of men among its brambles.
Northward, incessantly, the flickering gunnery
    rumbles,
Far off, like a dull rumour of some other war.
        What are we doing here?

The poignant misery of dawn begins to grow . . .
We only know war lasts, rain soaks, and clouds sag
    stormy.
Dawn massing in the east her melancholy army
Attacks once more in ranks on shivering ranks of grey,
        But nothing happens.

Sudden successive flights of bullets streak the silence.
Less deathly than the air that shudders black with
    snow,
With sidelong flowing flakes that flock, pause, and
    renew;
We watch them wandering up and down the wind's
    nonchalance,
        But nothing happens.

Pale flakes with fingering stealth come feeling for our
    faces –
We cringe in holes, back on forgotten dreams, and
    stare, snow-dazed,
Deep into grassier ditches. So we drowse, sun-dozed,
Littered with blossoms trickling where the blackbird
    fusses,
        – Is it that we are dying?

Slowly our ghosts drag home: glimpsing the sunk fires,
    glozed[2]
With crusted dark-red jewels; crickets jingle there;
For hours the innocent mice rejoice: the house is theirs;
Shutters and doors, all closed: on us the doors are
    closed, –
        We turn back to our dying.

Since we believe not otherwise can kind fires burn;
Nor ever suns smile true on child, or field, or fruit.
For God's invincible spring our love is made afraid;
Therefore, not loath, we lie out here; therefore were
born,
        For love of God seems dying.

Tonight, this frost will fasten on this mud and us,
Shrivelling many hands, puckering foreheads crisp.
The burying-party, picks and shovels in shaking grasp,
Pause over half-known faces. All their eyes are ice,
        But nothing happens.

WILFRED OWEN

[1] where the front line juts into enemy territory
[2] an invented word, mixing *glowing* and *glazed*

What are the soldiers doing? How does the short line 'But nothing happens' go against our usual idea of warfare?
Do the men feel winter or war is more dangerous to them? Which words and comparisons connect weather and war?
What sort of sounds does Owen include? How

do they help to make the atmosphere of the poem?

Which adjectives (descriptive words) do you find most vivid and exact?

Look at lines 3 and 4 of the third verse. Exactly what is compared to what?

Look at the line-end rhymes. They are strange (*knive us/nervous; silent/salient*). Owen invented these half-rhymes or para-rhymes. They give a tight shape to the verse while avoiding the bounciness of ordinary rhymes. Do you like them? Work out the other sets and say which work well and which do not.

As the soldiers grow numb with cold, strange pictures come into their minds. What are these? How do the daydreams end? What is sad about this?

In the seventh verse, the soldiers explain their reasons for fighting. What are these? Do you agree with the reasons?

Which words or phrases do you like in the later part of the poem: for example, the picture of the spring day or the sinking fire?

The poem ends with the sinister picture of the effects of cold on the battlefield. What job does the burying party have to do? Why is it so difficult?

Why is 'half-known faces' or 'All their eyes are ice' so powerful?

Would you say that this was an angry or a sad poem? Is it about protest or patriotism?

Edgell Rickword joined the army straight from school and lost an eye in fighting on the Western Front. He wrote a few poems after 1918, looking back on the war.

Winter Warfare

Colonel Cold strode up the Line
  (Tabs of rime and spurs of ice),
Stiffened all where he did glare,
  Horses, men, and lice.

Visited a forward post,
  Left them burning, ear to foot;
Fingers stuck to biting steel,
  Toes to frozen boot.

Stalked on into No Man's Land,
  Turned the wire to fleecy wool,
Iron stakes to sugar sticks
  Snapping at a pull.

Those who watched with hoary eyes
  Saw two figures gleaming there;
Hauptman Kälte, Colonel Cold,
  Gaunt, in the grey air.

Stiffly, tinkling spurs they moved
  Glassy eyed, with glinting heel
Stabbing those who lingered there
  Torn by screaming steel.

EDGELL RICKWORD

Why should a soldier connect winter and a senior officer? Do you find this effective?

Rickword uses some grim jokes. What are these?

In the last two verses, another figure, Hauptman Kälte, appears. What is the point of this?

The last two lines are particularly savage. What exactly is happening? What sad idea is expressed in the word 'linger'?

W Write about *Exposure*.
What scenes does it describe to us?
What are the various thoughts of the soldiers as they lie in the snow?
Which parts of the poem impress you most?
What do you like about the language of the poem?
Do you like the half-rhymes and the short lines at the end of each verse?
How does the poem differ from the usual picture of war?

W Write about the two poems together. Compare:
  the scenes they describe,
  the thoughts of the men in the trenches,
  the way that the horrors of war and winter are related,
  the choice of words and use of comparisons,
  the use of rhymes or varied line lengths.
Which poem do you like better?

A Bombing Post in the Snow: *John Nash*

W This painting is called *A Bombing Post in the Snow*. **It is by John Nash, who fought in France and Flanders. Write about the picture,** describing the thoughts of one of the soldiers in the shell-hole. Use detail from the picture but also include ideas from Owen's *Exposure*.

UNIT 14   *Disabled: a victim of war*

Wilfred Owen imagines the thoughts of a very young and severely wounded soldier. He has lost all of his limbs and now sits helplessly in a wheelchair, thinking sadly and bitterly of the past.

Disabled

He sat in a wheeled chair, waiting for dark,
And shivered in his ghastly suit of grey,
Legless, sewn short at elbow. Through the park
Voices of boys rang saddening like a hymn,
Voices of play and pleasure after day,
Till gathering sleep had mothered them from him.

*   *   *

About this time Town used to swing so gay
When glow-lamps budded in the light blue trees,
And girls glanced lovelier as the air grew dim, –
In the old times, before he threw away his knees.
Now he will never feel again how slim
Girls' waists are, or how warm their subtle hands;
All of them touch him like some queer disease.

*   *   *

There was an artist silly for his face,
For it was younger than his youth, last year.
Now, he is old; his back will never brace;
He's lost his colour very far from here,
Poured it down shell-holes till the veins ran dry,
And half his lifetime lapsed in the hot race
And leap of purple spurted from his thigh.

* * *

One time he liked a blood-smear down his leg,
After the matches, carried shoulder-high.
It was after football, when he'd drunk a peg,
He thought he'd better join. – He wonders why.
Someone had said he'd look a god in kilts,
That's why; and may be, too, to please his Meg;
Aye, that was it, to please the giddy jilts
He asked to join. He didn't have to beg;
Smiling they wrote his lie; aged nineteen years.
Germans he scarcely thought of; all their guilt,
And Austria's, did not move him. And no fears
Of Fear came yet. He thought of jewelled hilts
For daggers in plaid socks; of smart salutes;
And care of arms; and leave; and pay arrears;
Esprit de corps;[1] and hints for young recruits.
And soon, he was drafted out with drums and cheers.

* * *

Some cheered him home, but not as crowds cheer Goal.
Only a solemn man who brought him fruits
Thanked him; and then inquired about his soul.

* * *

Now, he will spend a few sick years in institutes,
And do what things the rules consider wise,
And take whatever pity they may dole.
To-night he noticed how the women's eyes
Passed from him to the strong men that were whole.
How cold and late it is! Why don't they come
And put him into bed? Why don't they come?

WILFRED OWEN

[1] soldierly spirit

Why is the wounded man waiting for dark?
What feelings and memories might the boys'
voices arouse in him?
What did he used to like and find exciting
about evenings just before the war?
What was he like then? What did he enjoy
doing before he joined the army?
How did women and girls treat him before the
war? How do they treat him now?
'One time he liked a blood-smear down his
leg': where and why? Why is this line a grim
joke? (Look at the previous three lines.)
Why did he join the army? What did he ignore
about war when he enlisted?

What lie did he tell to the recruiting
sergeants? Why did they smile?
What was the difference between 'cheering
Goal' and 'cheering him home'?
What is his future?
What is Owen angry about in this poem?

W Write your own story of this young victim,
using details from the poem. Describe his life
before the war, why he joined up, how he was
wounded, and what happened to him
afterwards.

W Imagine that Meg visits him in hospital.
What do they say to each other? (Bring in the
pre-war memories.)
What are their thoughts about each other?
Will Meg keep up the relationship or
abandon the young soldier?
Use plenty of detail from the poem.

W Look at this picture of wounded men in
Brighton in 1916: the hospital there
specialized in limb injuries and amputations.
Imagine the thoughts of the girl, and the
mother, about the men.
What are the men's thoughts about the child/
their war service/their previous lives?

Wounded British soldiers on a Brighton sea-front, 1916

UNIT 15   *Commanding officers*

. . . With our old commander
Safely in the rear.

Soldiers' song

The much-criticized generals of the First World War tended to be elderly men who had grown up in the cavalry-dominated armies of the late-nineteenth century. They did not understand the new technology that had led to the stalemate of the trenches, and their dream was always to smash a hole in the line so that the cavalry could go through to restore open warfare. Meanwhile, in their bloody attempts to break the German Front, they were content, in Winston Churchill's words, 'to fight machine-gun bullets with the breasts of gallant men'. Moreover, they and their Staff officers lived in comfortable headquarters far from the Front. They understood little of local conditions as they drew up their battle plans.

The war correspondent, Philip Gibbs, wrote bitterly about Field Marshal Douglas Haig's Headquarters at Montreuil, which he called 'a City of Beautiful Nonsense'.

> One came to GHQ from journeys over the wild desert of the battlefields, where men lived in ditches, muddy, miserable in all things but spirit, as to a place where the pageantry of war still maintained its old and dead tradition. . . . It was as though men were playing at war here, while others, sixty miles away, were fighting and dying, in mud and gas waves and explosive barrages. . . .
>
> Often one saw the Commander-in-chief starting for an afternoon ride, a fine figure, nobly mounted, with an escort of Lancers. A pretty sight, with fluttering pennons on all their lances, and horses groomed to the last hair. It was prettier than the real thing up in the Salient or beyond the Somme, where dead bodies lay in upheaved earth among ruins and slaughtered trees. . . . Such careless-hearted courage when British soldiers were being blown to bits, gassed, blinded, maimed and shell-shocked in places that were far – so very far – from GHQ!

Philip Gibbs, *Realities of War*

Bad leadership is a key idea in soldier poetry. In *The General*, Siegfried Sassoon made the classic statement about the conduct of the War. In only seven lines, he summed up the bitterness of the fighting troops. He had himself fought in the Battles of the Somme (1916) and Arras (1917), and knew their terrible human cost.

The General

'Good-morning; good-morning!' the General said
When we met him last week on our way to the line.
Now the soldiers he smiled at are most of 'em dead,
And we're cursing his staff for incompetent swine.
'He's a cheery old card,'[1] grunted Harry to Jack
As they slogged up to Arras with rifle and pack.

*

But he did for them both by his plan of attack.

SIEGFRIED SASSOON

[1] smart fellow

How does the General's greeting contrast with the work that the men are about to do?
What happened to the soldiers? Who was to blame for their fate? Why mention Harry and Jack particularly?
The poem ends with three rhymes. What is the effect of the long pause before the last rhymed line?
The poem uses words from soldiers' slang and everyday conversation. Why? Do you think they are effective and add to the force of the poem?

A.P. Herbert fought at Gallipoli and the Somme and was severely wounded in 1917. His favourite themes in his fine war novel, *The Secret Battle*, and his angry war poems are the courage of his comrades and his contempt for those who controlled the fighting.

After the Battle

So they are satisfied with our Brigade,
　And it remains to parcel out the bays![1]
And we shall have the usual Thanks Parade,
　The beaming General, and the soapy praise.

You will come up in your capricious[2] car
　To find your heroes sulking in the rain,
To tell us how magnificent we are,
　And how you hope we'll do the same again.

And we, who knew your old abusive tongue,
  Who heard you hector us a week before,
We who have bled to boost you up a rung –
  A K.C.B. perhaps, perhaps a Corps –

We who must mourn those spaces in the mess,
  And somehow fill those hollows in the heart,
We do not want your Sermon on Success,
  Your greasy benisons[3] on Being Smart.

We only want to take our wounds away.
  To some warm village where the tumult ends,
And drowsing in the sunshine many a day,
  Forget our aches, forget that we had friends.

Weary we are of blood and noise and pain;
  This was a week we shall not soon forget;
And if, indeed, we have to fight again,
  We little wish to think about it yet.

We have done well; we like to hear it said.
  Say it, and then, for God's sake, say no more.
Fight, if you must, fresh battles far ahead,
  But keep them dark behind your chateau[4] door!

A.P. HERBERT

[1] rewards for victory (laurel wreaths)
[2] come at any time, keeping troops waiting
[3] blessings
[4] French mansion HQ

What does the writer hate about the General?
How does he behave before and after the battle?
What will he gain from the soldiers' victory?
What do the men want to do after the battle?
What was the worst part of their battle experience?
How do they see the future?

D Look at these two pictures. What do they tell us about the generals of the First World War?

A German cartoon mocking British leadership on the Somme, 1916

Field-Marshall Haig inspects his men

Godfrey Elton fought in the Middle East and was held prisoner by the Turks. He wrote several poems looking back on the conduct of the war.

The Survivor

I found him in department C.O.10.
Three rows of medals, D.S.O., C.B.,
Brown, handsome, fearless, born to handle men:
Brushed, buttoned, spurred. Whom did I wish to see?

'Men you can't send for, General,' I said,
'How great soever your expense of ink;
Men you've forgotten; the unribboned dead
Who fell because you were too brave to think.'

GODFREY ELTON

Why include the department number?
Elton dwells on the appearance of the General. Why is this?
With whom is the General contrasted?
Why are the dead 'unribboned'?
What is the force of the last line?

What is Elton's target in this angry poem?
The poem is very like Sassoon's *The General.* **Which do you prefer?**

W **What would the General in** *After the Battle* **think about after the trench victory?**
Write some of his thoughts in a paragraph. Then write a second contrasting paragraph giving Herbert's views of the battle and of the General.

W **Write about the three poems, outlining the ideas that they contain and comparing their language and styles. Which do you think is the best?**

W **Imagine that you are a general with a teenage son. Write him a letter describing your work in France and your feelings about the war and the men who fight for you.**
One of the general's men also has a son. Now write this man's letter home, describing your view of the conduct of the war and your own experience of army leadership.
Use plenty of detail from the extract and poems given here.

UNIT 16 *Death at the Front*

The First World War killed millions of people. Three quarters of a million men from Britain died; another one and a half million were seriously wounded. Death could be horribly swift or it could be slow and lingering for wounded men trapped in No Man's Land or caught in the barbed-wire.

In the early years of the war, before the mass slaughter of the great battles, it was consoling to think of death as a noble sacrifice. Herbert Asquith wrote about a military funeral.

The Fallen Subaltern

The starshells float above, the bayonets glisten;
   We bear our fallen friend without a sound;
Below the waiting legions lie and listen
   To us, who march upon their burial ground.

Wound in the flag of England, here we lay him;
   The guns will flash and thunder o'er the grave;
What other winding sheet should now array him,
   What other music should salute the brave?

As goes the Sun-God in his chariot glorious,
   When all his golden banners are unfurled,
So goes the soldier, fallen but victorious,
   And leaves behind a twilight in the world.

And those, who come this way in days hereafter,
   Will know that here a boy for England fell,
Who looked at danger with the eyes of laughter,
   And on the charge his days were ended well.

One last salute; the bayonets clash and glisten;
   The shadowy file goes by without a sound:
One more has found the men who lie and listen
   To us, who march upon their burial ground.

HERBERT ASQUITH

Who are the waiting legions of the first and last verses?
Although they are dead, what qualities are they given?
To what is the dead soldier compared?

How did the soldier die? Why?
How does the poet feel about the death of this young man?

Wilfred Owen's *Futility*, about one dead soldier, may be based on his first spell in the battle line in January 1917: 'The marvel is that we did not all die of cold. As a matter of fact, only one of my party actually froze to death before he could be got back.' Or the dead man may have been a sudden casualty shot down by a sniper at dawn. The poem begins with a crazy order to put the body in the sunshine: somehow the sun might bring him back to life.

Futility

Move him into the sun –
Gently its touch awoke him once,
At home, whispering of fields half-sown.
Always it woke him, even in France,
Until this morning and this snow.
If anything might rouse him now
The kind old sun will know.

Think how it wakes the seeds –
Woke once the clays of a cold star.
Are limbs, so dear achieved, are sides
Full-nerved, still warm, too hard to stir?
Was it for this the clay grew tall?
– O what made fatuous sunbeams toil
To break earth's sleep at all?

WILFRED OWEN

A Death Among the Wounded in the Snow: *William Orpen*

What work did the dead soldier do before the war? Why, therefore, should the sun wake him?
'Fields half-sown': what point is made here about the man, his life, and his work?
The 'kind old sun' is the centre of the poem. What wonderful things has it created on the 'cold star' (planet Earth)?
Owen looks closely at the dead man. Why are his limbs 'dear achieved'?
The body is 'still warm' and 'full-nerved': why do these give Owen a kind of hope?
In the line, 'Was it for this the clay grew tall?', Owen is thinking of the biblical story

of Adam's creation: 'Then the Lord formed a man from the dust of the ground'. What, then, does this line mean?

Realizing that the man is finally, hopelessly dead, Owen asks an angry question in the last two lines. What is this?

Do you like the half-rhymes in this poem? Why does Owen use them here?

Having looked at these details, think about the whole poem. What does Owen feel about the death of this man?

W Write a commentary on this poem. What happens in it? What are Owen's thoughts about what happens? What features of the poem – words, comparisons, shape – do you find interesting?

W Compare the two poems. Think about the stories that they tell, the writers' attitudes to death in war, and the style and language used. Which do you prefer and why?

W Look at the painting on page 55 by William Orpen called *A Death Among the Wounded in the Snow*. Write a story or description based on it. Try to bring in thoughts and ideas from Owen's *Futility*.

UNIT 17   *Sassoon's rebellion*

Siegfried Sassoon was a gallant officer, who won the Military Cross for courage and fought at several battles, yet he also detested the slaughter and the misconduct of the war by generals and politicians. His protest took two forms: his celebrated statement against the war, which was published in *The Times*, and his deadly, satirical war poems, which he called 'trench rockets sent up to illuminate the gloom'. Winston Churchill called them 'cries of pain wrung from soldiers during a test to destruction'.

Sassoon came from a wealthy banking family. After studying at Cambridge, he was able to live without a profession and devoted himself to hunting, riding and cricket, and to poetry, which he published at his own expense.
    When war came, he quickly volunteered and became an officer in the Royal Welch Fusiliers. His war diary recorded his experiences of the Front.

If you search carefully, you may find a skull, eyeless, grotesquely matted with what was once hair; eyes once looked from these detestable holes . . . they were lit with triumph and beautiful with pity . . .
                                        30 March 1916

In July 1916, he took part in the murderous opening of the Battle of the Somme.

The dead are terrible and undignified carcasses, stiff and contorted . . . some side by side on their backs with bloody clotted fingers mingled as if they were hand-shaking in the companionship of death. And the stench undefinable. And rags and shreds of blood-stained cloth, bloody boots riddled and torn . . .
                                        14 July 1916

On leave after illness, he began his first anti-war poems, later published in *The Old Huntsman* (1917). In 1917, he returned to France and fought in the Battle of Arras.

Two mud-stained hands were sticking out of the wet, ashen, chalky soil, like the roots of a shrub turned upside down. They might have been imploring; they might have been groping and struggling for life and release: but the dead man was hidden; he was buried . . .
                                        19 April 1917

Gas attack: from Der Krieg *by Otto Dix*

Sassoon was wounded and sent home. In a London hospital, he was haunted by hideous dreams about the war.

> When the lights are out, and the ward is half shadow . . . then the horrors come creeping across the floor; the floor is littered with parcels of dead flesh and bones, faces glaring at the ceiling . . . hands clutching neck or belly . . .
>
> 23 April 1917

In June 1917, he began his personal crusade against the fighting, influenced both by his own experiences and by the writing of Pacifists such as Bertrand Russell. Refusing military duties, he sent this protest statement to his commanding officer and to the press.

> I am making this statement as an act of wilful defiance of military authority, because I believe that the War is being deliberately prolonged by those who have the power to end it. I am a soldier, convinced that I am acting on behalf of soldiers. I believe that this War, upon which I entered as a war of defence and liberation, has now become a war of aggression and conquest. I believe that the purposes for which I and my fellow-soldiers entered upon this War should have been so clearly stated as to have made it impossible for them to be changed without our knowledge, and that, had this been done, the object which actuated us would now be attainable by negotiation.
>
> I have seen and endured the sufferings of the troops, and I can no longer be a party to prolonging those sufferings for ends which I believe to be evil and unjust.
>
> I am not protesting against the military conduct of the War, but against the political errors and insincerities for which the fighting men are being sacrificed.
>
> On behalf of those who are suffering now, I make this protest against the deception which is being practised on them. Also I believe that it may help to destroy the callous complacence with which the majority of those at home regard the continuance of agonies which they do not share, and which they have not sufficient imagination to realise.

What are Sassoon's objections to the conduct of the war in 1917?
Who are the chief victims of the war?
Who is the most to blame for the continuation of the war?
Do you think a soldier should have published such a statement?

In Liverpool, while Sassoon's case was being discussed, he tore the Military Cross ribbon from his tunic and threw it into the River Mersey. He was declared shell-shocked and was sent to Craiglockhart Hospital in Edinburgh. There he wrote more poems which were collected in *Counter-Attack* (1918).

Siegfried Sassoon, painted in summer 1917, at the time of his protest against the war

In 1918, Sassoon returned to active service, first in the Middle East and then in France. On patrol in No Man's Land, he was shot and wounded by one of his own men. In this strange way, he escaped from the Front and survived the war, living on until 1967.

Sassoon's poems aimed to tell the truth about war. He particularly wanted to upset 'blood-thirsty civilians and those who falsely glorified the war'. Memories from France and hints from newspapers would 'bring poems into my head as though from nowhere'. He used a plain, direct style, often bringing in soldiers' slang. A pattern of sharp lines often leads to a 'knock-out blow' in the last verse.

An early success was *Died of Wounds*, based on a dying soldier whom he saw in a hospital near the Somme in July 1916.

Gassed and Wounded: *Eric Kennington*

Died of Wounds

His wet white face and miserable eyes
Brought nurses to him more than groans and sighs:
But hoarse and low and rapid rose and fell
His troubled voice: he did the business well.

The ward grew dark; but he was still complaining
And calling out for 'Dickie'. 'Curse the Wood!
It's time to go. O Christ, and what's the good?
We'll never take it, and it's always raining.'

I wondered where he'd been; then heard him shout,
'They snipe like hell! O Dickie, don't go out'. . . .
I fell asleep. . . . Next morning he was dead;
And some Slight Wound lay smiling on the bed.

> **Who was Dickie? Why is the dying man so
> distressed about him?**
> **Which two lines best express the horror and
> futility of war?**
> **What is the sad meaning of the last line?**

In *The Hero*, Sassoon offers us a bitter contrast
between a mother's view of her dead son and the
opinions of his fellow officers. A 'brother officer'
has gone to her home to tell her how her son died.

The Hero

'Jack fell as he'd have wished,' the Mother said,
And folded up the letter that she'd read.
'The Colonel writes so nicely.' Something broke
In the tired voice that quavered to a choke.
She half looked up. 'We mothers are so proud
Of our dead soldiers.' Then her face was bowed.

Quietly the Brother Officer went out.
He'd told the poor old dear some gallant lies
That she would nourish all her days, no doubt.
For while he coughed and mumbled, her weak eyes
Had shone with gentle triumph, brimmed with joy,
Because he'd been so brave, her glorious boy.

He thought how 'Jack', cold-footed, useless swine,
Had panicked down the trench that night the mine
Went up at Wicked Corner; how he'd tried
To get sent home, and how, at last, he died,
Blown to small bits. And no one seemed to care
Except that lonely woman with white hair.

> **What is the mother's reaction to the letter?
> How had Jack actually behaved at the Front?
> How does the 'brother officer' feel about his
> visit? What had he done to help the mother?
> Sassoon uses two kinds of language about the
> war. What are the differences?**
>
> **W** **Imagine that you are the 'brother officer'.
> Write a letter to a friend about this visit.
> Include the mother's reactions and make more
> of Jack's actual behaviour at the Front.**

'Base details' were men who worked at supply
depots well away from the Front Line.

Base Details

If I were fierce, and bald, and short of breath,
    I'd live with scarlet Majors at the Base,
And speed glum heroes up the line to death.
    You'd see me with my puffy petulant face
Guzzling and gulping in the best hotel,
    Reading the Roll of Honour. 'Poor young chap',
I'd say – 'I used to know his father well:
    Yes, we've lost heavily in this last scrap.'
And when the war is done and youth stone dead,
I'd toddle safely home and die – in bed.

> **What other meaning is included in the title?
> What does the typical senior officer look like
> and how does he behave?
> What two meanings are there in 'scarlet
> Majors'?
> What is the point of the last two lines?
> Sassoon is very good at choosing precise words.
> Which do you find most vivid?**

Self-inflicted wounds or suicide were desperate
forms of escape from the horrors of the trenches.

Suicide in the Trenches

I knew a simple soldier boy
Who grinned at life in empty joy,
Slept soundly through the lonesome dark,
And whistled early with the lark.

In winter trenches, cowed and glum,
With crumps[1] and lice and lack of rum,
He put a bullet through his brain.
No one spoke of him again.

      *   *   *

You smug-faced crowds with kindling eye
Who cheer when soldier lads march by,
Sneak home and pray you'll never know
The hell where youth and laughter go.

[1] shell bursts

What sort of person was the young soldier?
Do you find it surprising that he should break down?
What contributed to his collapse?
Why did 'no one speak of him again'?
Who is the target for Sassoon's anger in the last verse?
Do you find the pauses effective here?
This is a simple but precise poem. Which words are well chosen? Why is the brilliant last line so forceful?

Sassoon looks at various terrible injuries caused by war.

Does it Matter?

Does it matter? – losing your legs? . . .
For people will always be kind,
And you need not show that you mind
When the others come in after hunting
To gobble their muffins and eggs.

Does it matter? – losing your sight? . . .
There's such splendid work for the blind;
And people will always be kind,
As you sit on the terrace remembering
And turning your face to the light.

Do they matter? – those dreams from the pit? . . .
You can drink and forget and be glad,
And people won't say that you're mad;
For they'll know that you've fought for your country
And no one will worry a bit.

What are the injuries? Which do you think is worst?
Sassoon uses sarcasm to sharp effect here: for example, 'There's such splendid work for the blind'. What does Sassoon really mean?
Which verse is most striking?
What attitudes is Sassoon attacking in this poem?

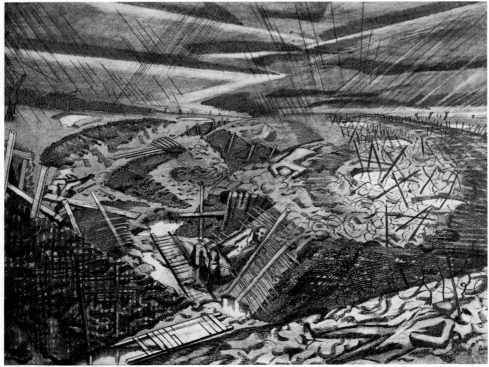

After the Battle: *Paul Nash*

Great Men

The great ones of the earth
Approve, with smiles and bland salutes, the rage
And monstrous tyranny they have brought to birth.
The great ones of the earth
Are much concerned about the wars they wage,
And quite aware of what those wars are worth.

You Marshals, gilt and red,
You Ministers and Princes, and Great Men,
Why can't you keep your mouthings for the dead?
Go round the simple cemeteries; and then
Talk of our noble sacrifice and losses
To the wooden crosses.

Who exactly are the 'Great Men' that Sassoon is writing about?

What does he hate about them?
What are their 'mouthings'?
Contrasts are used strongly here. Which are effective?
Do you find the last two lines forceful? What do they tell us?

W **Write about Sassoon's poetic protest against the First World War. You will need a brief introduction: you could use the protest statement there. Then write about some or all of the poems here, and consider some of the outstanding themes. Look at his rhymes, comparisons, and precise word choice, and say how these contribute to the protest. End by saying which poem you find the most impressive.**

UNIT 18   *Wilfred Owen at Craiglockhart*

Owen is now seen as the most important of the many poets of the First World War. A recent critic says of his poems: 'They speak to our world still, as they were meant to do. . . . He has done as much as anyone to prevent the reading public from being persuaded ever again that death in battle is "sweet and decorous".'

The son of a railway worker, Owen was born in Shropshire and educated at schools in Shrewsbury and Liverpool. His devoted mother encouraged his early interests in music and poetry. When he could not afford a university education, he went abroad to teach English in France. He was there when war broke out in 1914. He wrote a draft for a war poem that contrasted strangely with his later work. This is part of it.

from: **The Ballad of Peace and War**

Oh meet it is and passing sweet
    To live at peace with others,
But sweeter still and far more meet
    To die in war for brothers . . .

The soil is safe, for widow and waif,
    And for the soul of England,
Because their bodies men vouchsafe
    To save the soul of England.

He returned to England to volunteer for the army, telling his mother, 'I now do most intensely want to fight'. After training, he became an officer and was sent to France at the end of 1916, seeing service first in the Somme sector. In spring 1917, he took part in the attacks on the German Hindenburg Line near St Quentin. When a huge shell burst near him, he was shell-shocked and sent back to England.

The horrors of battle had changed him quickly from the youth of August 1914, who had felt that 'the guns will effect a little useful weeding'. Now he wrote to his mother:

> Already I have comprehended a light which never will filter into the dogma of any national church: namely that one of Christ's essential commands was: Passivity at any price! Suffer dishonour and disgrace; but never resort to arms. Be bullied, be outraged, be killed: but do not kill.
>
> 16 May 1917

Owen was treated at Craiglockhart Hospital in Edinburgh. Doctors there specialized in shell-shock. By day it was cheerful enough but at night the officer patients were tormented by their memories.

> One lay awake and listened to feet padding along passages which smelt of stale cigarette smoke. . .

one became conscious that the place was full of men whose slumbers were morbid and terrifying – men muttering uneasily or suddenly crying out in their sleep . . . by night each man was back in his doomed sector of a horror-stricken Front Line, where the panic and stampede of some ghastly experience was re-enacted among the livid faces of the dead. No doctor could save him then . . .

Siegfried Sassoon, *Sherston's Progress*

Patients were encouraged to return to their pre-war interests. Owen looked over his old poems and began to write new ones. He read Sassoon's *The Old Huntsman* and was deeply impressed. It was a great moment for him when Sassoon himself arrived at the Hospital in August 1917. He plucked up the courage to visit him. Sassoon recalled the first meeting.

One morning at the beginning of August, when I had been at Craiglockhart War Hospital about a fortnight, there was a gentle knock on the door of my room and a young officer entered. Short, dark-haired, and shyly hesitant, he stood for a moment before coming across to the window, where I was sitting on my bed cleaning my golf clubs. A favourable first impression was made by the fact that he had under his arm several copies of *The Old Huntsman*. He had come, he said, hoping that I would be so gracious as to inscribe them for himself and some of his friends. He spoke with a slight stammer, which was no unusual thing in that neurosis-pervaded hospital. . . .

During the next half-hour or more I must have spoken mainly about my book and its interpretations of the War. He listened eagerly, questioning me with reticent intelligence. It was only when he was departing that he confessed to being a writer of poetry himself, though none of it had yet appeared in print.

It amuses me to remember that, when I had resumed my ruminative club-polishing, I wondered whether his poems were any good! He had seemed an interesting little chap but had not struck me as remarkable. In fact my first view of him was as a rather ordinary young man.

Siegfried Sassoon, *Siegfried's Journey*

Sassoon encouraged Owen in his writing, telling him to 'sweat your guts out writing poetry'. When Owen began to write new poems based on his war experiences, Sassoon helped him to improve and develop his drafts.

Anthem for Doomed Youth was an example of their collaboration.

Anthem for Doomed Youth

What passing-bells for these who die as cattle?
  – Only the monstrous anger of the guns.
  Only the stuttering rifles' rapid rattle
Can patter out their hasty orisons.[1]
No mockeries now for them; no prayers nor bells;
  Nor any voice of mourning save the choirs, –
The shrill, demented[2] choirs of wailing shells;
  And bugles calling for them from sad shires.

What candles may be held to speed them all?
  Not in the hands of boys but in their eyes
Shall shine the holy glimmers of goodbyes.
  The pallor of girls' brows shall be their pall;[3]
Their flowers the tenderness of patient[4] minds,
And each slow dusk a drawing-down of blinds.

[1] prayers	[3] cloth to cover coffin
[2] mad	[4] suffering

The poem is a sonnet, a favourite form of Owen. There are 14 lines; each line has five stressed syllables, and the lines end in rhymes in this pattern: ABABCDCD EFFEGG.

The poem is a long comparison between the elaborate ceremonial of a Victorian-style funeral and the way in which men go to death on the Western Front.
What is the counterpart in the trenches of each of these ceremonial details:
   passing (funeral) bell,
   prayers,
   church choir,
   funeral candles,
   pall,
   flowers,
   drawing down blinds in a house in mourning?

Owen was a fine musician with an acute ear for the texture of words. In which lines does he use the sound of words to imitate what he is describing (a technique known as *onomatopoeia*)?

Does Owen like funeral ceremonial? Which word tells you his opinion?
Do you think the elaborate comparisons make the poem more or less powerful as a comment on war?

D Here are two of the drafts (first versions) of the poem.
Study them carefully and compare them with the final version. Discuss the changes, in particular why:
  monstrous is better than *solemn*,
  doomed is better than *dead*,
  patient is better than the several other ideas,
  each slow is better than *every* dusk.
Consider the changes in complete lines, too.

W Write about *Anthem for Doomed Youth*. Say what the poem is about and what it tells us about soldiers at the Front and people at home in Britain. Comment on the words, sounds of words, and comparisons that Owen uses. Use some of the detailed ideas mentioned above.

Two drafts of Anthem for Doomed Youth *by Wilfred Owen*

Anthem for Dead Youth.

Anthem for ~~Dead~~ doomed Youth –   N. F.

What passing-bells for these who die as cattle?
  – Only the monstrous anger of the guns.
  Only the stuttering rifles' rapid rattle
Can patter out their hasty orisons.
No {mockeries ~~music for all them~~; ~~no~~ nor no} prayers nor bells,
  Nor any voice of mourning save the choirs,
The shrill ~~demented~~ ented choirs of wailing shells;
  And bugles calling ~~sad~~ ~~across the~~ for them from sad shires.

What candles may be held to speed them all?
  Not in the hands of boys, but in their eyes
Shall shine the holy glimmers of goodbyes.
And The pallor of girl's brows shall be their pall;
  Their flowers the tenderness of {~~silent~~ patient} minds,
And each slow dusk a drawing-down of blinds.

(Pencil words were written by
S.S. when W. showed him the
sonnet at Craiglockhart in
Sept. 1917.)

Another of Owen's Craiglockhart poems was *Dulce et Decorum Est*, which has become one of the best-known poems of the twentieth century. In a letter to his mother he wrote:

> Here is a gas poem, done yesterday. . . . The famous Latin tag means of course *It is sweet and meet to die for one's country. Sweet!* And *decorous!*

16 October 1917

The 'tag' was from a poem by the Roman poet, Horace, and was much quoted during the days of the British Empire in the nineteenth century, during the Boer War, and also after 1914. Owen attacks the sentimental, bogus patriotism of stay-at-home war enthusiasts: the poem was first addressed to Jessie Pope (see p.33). She is the 'you' of the last section of the poem.

Dulce et Decorum est

Bent double, like old beggars under sacks,
Knock-kneed, coughing like hags, we cursed through
  sludge,
Till on the haunting flares we turned our backs
And towards our distant rest began to trudge.
Men marched asleep. Many had lost their boots
But limped on, blood-shod. All went lame; all blind;
Drunk with fatigue; deaf even to the hoots
Of tired, outstripped Five-Nines that dropped behind.

Gas! GAS! Quick, boys! – An ecstasy of fumbling,
Fitting the clumsy helmets just in time;
But someone still was yelling out and stumbling,
And flound'ring like a man in fire or lime . . .
Dim, through the misty panes and thick green light,
As under a green sea, I saw him drowning.

In all my dreams, before my helpless sight,
He plunges at me, guttering, choking, drowning.

If in some smothering dreams you too could pace
Behind the wagon that we flung him in,
And watch the white eyes writhing in his face,
His hanging face, like a devil's sick of sin;
If you could hear, at every jolt, the blood
Come gargling from the froth-corrupted lungs,
Obscene as cancer, bitter as the cud
Of vile, incurable sores on innocent tongues, –
My friend, you would not tell with such high zest
To children ardent for some desperate glory,
The old Lie: Dulce et decorum est
Pro patria mori.

In the first section, British soldiers are leaving the trenches after an exhausting span of duty. They stagger back to rest areas. The soldiers are compared to two surprising things. What are they?

Owen uses many words which are ugly in texture: pick out some of these.

What does 'blood-shod' mean?

In the second section, green fumes of poison gas spread round the men.

What strange comparison is used to describe them in the gas?

Why does one man die? What do the others do with him?

The last section contains some hideous comparisons. What is compared to what in these phrases:
  like a devil's sick of sin,
  bitter as the cud of vile, incurable sores on
    innocent tongues, . . . ?

Why does Owen hate 'my friend'? What exactly is his message for her?

D Sassoon and Owen worked together on the poem. One of several drafts is shown on the page opposite. Compare it with the final version, looking in particular at:
  haunting **rather than** *clawing,*
  guttering **rather than** *gurgling,*
  the comparison of the dead soldier's face to
    a rose,
  the completely recast sections.

British casualties of gas attacks: Gassed *by John Singer Sargent*

W Write about *Dulce et Decorum Est*. **What story does it tell?**
What conclusions does Owen draw from this story as a message to war enthusiasts in Britain?
Which words and comparisons do you find especially forceful and interesting?

W Recast the material in the poem into a letter written by Owen to a friend at home. Try to include the 'story' of the poem, its angry theme, and some of the force and indignation of its language.

Draft of **Dulce et Decorum est** *by Wilfred Owen*

W **Devise a script or role play based on the meeting of Wilfred Owen and Siegfried Sassoon. They might discuss their own backgrounds, the war and their parts in it, their poems. They might discuss** Anthem for Doomed Youth: **use the manuscript given on p.62.**

Wilfred Owen in July 1916

UNIT 19 *Anger and satire*

After 1916, the huge casualty lists, the introduction of conscription, and the poor quality of military and political leadership produced much protest against the war by civilian and soldier writers. Official censorship tried but failed to silence them. Satire was their most deadly weapon: a bitter, mocking laughter directed against authority, arm-chair civilian warriors, lying propaganda, or the insanity and waste of war itself. Edward Garnett wrote prose satire which was typical of the later years of the war.

What a wonderful time the Creatures of Blood were having all over Europe! Never in the story of man . . . had there been such slaughter, havoc, massacre, insanity, famine and the abomination of desolation on this planet, on as gigantic a scale, as in these glorious years. . . . The Creatures of Blood in every belligerent country, who had so long grown fat on peace and still supped on plenty, rubbed their white podgy hands, while their bloodshot elderly eyes glanced through the newspapers which bawled night and morning everywhere for bigger and bigger armies to wade deeper and deeper into the morass of European slaughter . . .

Edward Garnett, *Papa's War and Other Essays*

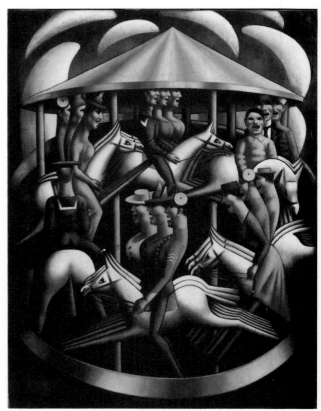

In Mark Gertler's protest painting, **The Merry-go-round** *(1916), war-crazed civilians and soldiers circle pointlessly, chanting crude patriotic slogans*

W.N. Ewer was a socialist. Hopes had been expressed just after the outbreak of war that working men in all combatant countries might remember their international brotherhood and unite to stop the fighting. However, in this 1914 poem, Ewer sees the working class of Europe as victims of propaganda.

Five Souls

FIRST SOUL
I was a peasant of the Polish plain;
I left my plough because the message ran:
Russia, in danger, needed every man
To save her from the Teuton; and was slain.
I gave my life for freedom – This I know
For those who bade me fight had told me so.

SECOND SOUL
I was a Tyrolese, a mountaineer;
I gladly left my mountain home to fight
Against the brutal treacherous Muscovite;
And died in Poland on a cossack spear.
I gave my life for freedom – This I know
For those who bade me fight had told me so.

THIRD SOUL
I worked in Lyons at my weaver's loom,
When suddenly the Prussian despot hurled
His felon blow at France and at the world;
Then I went forth to Belgium and my doom.
I gave my life for freedom – This I know
For those who bade me fight had told me so.

FOURTH SOUL
I owned a vineyard by the wooded Main,
Until the Fatherland, begirt by foes
Lusting her downfall, called me, and I rose
Swift to the call – and died in far Lorraine.
I gave my life for freedom – This I know
For those who bade me fight had told me so.

FIFTH SOUL
I worked in a great shipyard by the Clyde;
There came a sudden word of wars declared,
Of Belgium, peaceful, helpless, unprepared,
Asking our aid; I joined the ranks, and died.
I gave my life for freedom – This I know
For those who bade me fight had told me so.

W.N. EWER

What is the effect of the repeated chorus in each verse?
Which words from official propaganda does Ewer put into the mouths of his working men?
Who, in Ewer's opinion, are the real enemies of these men?
Do you agree, or disagree, with the poet?

Harold Begbie, a convinced Christian, lost his early enthusiasm for the war (see p.32). He came to detest the attitudes of the right-wing press, especially the notion that war was 'good' for people.

War Exalts

War exalts and cleanses: it lifts man from the mud!
Ask God what He thinks of a bayonet dripping blood.

By War the brave are tested, and cowards are disgraced!
Show God His own image shrapnel'd into paste.

Fight till tyrants perish, slay till brutes are mild!
Then go wash the blood off and try to face your child.

HAROLD BEGBIE

Each verse consists of a statement praising war, and an answer attacking it. What are the statements and what are Begbie's answers? His answers are blunt and vivid. Which do you find most striking?

Those who sit in the high places cast the people into the pit

The soldier as the victim of forces in society who profit from war: cartoon by Joseph Southall

H. Smalley Sarson served in the ranks, sending home his poems to be published. He takes the flight of a single shell as a particular example of the pointless waste and destruction of battle.

The Shell

Shrieking its message the flying death
    Cursed the resisting air,
Then buried its nose by a battered church,
    A skeleton gaunt and bare.

The brains of science, the money of fools
    Had fashioned an iron slave
Destined to kill, yet the futile end
    Was a child's uprooted grave.

H. SMALLEY SARSON

Which words in the first two lines make the shell sound fearsome and impressive?
What efforts had gone into the making of the shell?
What damage did it actually do?
Do you like the simplicity and directness of the poem?

'To your health, civilization!': in this cartoon by Louis Raemaekers, Death celebrates the slaughter of 1916 with a toast drunk in blood

In a tiny poem, Israel Zangwill summed up the state of Europe in one of the blackest of the war years, 1916, when the destructive battles of Verdun and the Somme were fought.

1916

The world bloodily-minded,
    The church dead or polluted,
The blind leading the blinded,
    And the deaf dragging the muted.

ISRAEL ZANGWILL

What does 'The church dead or polluted' mean?
The 'blind', 'deaf', and 'muted' are not war wounded.
Who, then, are the 'blind' and the 'blinded'?
Who are the 'deaf'?
In what sense are the 'muted' silent?
What does Zangwill find most disturbing about the world of 1916?

Britain relied on volunteers for its army until 1916, when conscription (compulsory military service) was introduced. In *The Conscript*, Wilfrid Gibson imagines recruits parading for their medical test, watched by casual doctors who have to choose those who are to go to war and those who are not.

The Conscript

Indifferent, flippant, earnest, but all bored,
The doctors sit in the glare of electric light
Watching the endless stream of naked white
Bodies of men for whom their hasty award
Means life or death maybe, or the living death
Of mangled limbs, blind eyes, or a darkened brain;
And the chairman, as his monocle falls again,
Pronounces each doom with easy indifferent breath.

Then suddenly I shudder as I see
A young man stand before them wearily,
Cadaverous[1] as one already dead;
But still they stare untroubled as he stands
With arms outstretched and drooping thorn-crowned
    head,
The nail-marks glowing in his feet and hands.

WILFRID GIBSON

[1] corpse-like

Which words and details describe the doctors and their attitude to their job?

Why does Gibson hate them?

What does their 'hasty award' (*fit* or *unfit*) mean to the recruits?

Gibson focuses on one man. The man reminds him of someone, indeed he actually seems to be that person. Who is this?

Do you like this last section? How does it compare to the powerful first part of the poem?

The dance of Death: a protest against various corrupt elements in European Society that were profiting from the war

Several poets saw a gulf between the generations: while young men died, the older generation – politicians, businessmen, army commanders – seemed to do very well out of the war.

Thomas Burke was known for his poems and stories about the poor in London's East End. Here he imagines the thoughts of an old Chinese immigrant who observes our society as an outsider.

Of the Great White War

During the years when the white men fought each
   other,
I observed how the aged cried aloud in public places
Of honour and chivalry, and the duty of the young;
And how the young ceased doing the pleasant things of
   youth,
And became suddenly old,
And marched away to defend the aged.
And I observed how the aged
Became suddenly young;
And mouthed fair phrases one to the other upon the
   Supreme Sacrifice,
And turned to their account books, murmuring gravely:
Business as Usual;
And brought out the bottles of wine and drank the
   health
Of the young men they had sent out to die for them.

THOMAS BURKE

Why did the young become 'suddenly old'?
How did the older generation turn 'suddenly young'?
What various things did the Chinese man hate about the older men?
Why did they drink the health of young soldiers?

A cartoon by Herbert Cole from an anti-war magazine, The Labour Leader, *1918*

Losses were so heavy that some fighting men began to see the war as a kind of plot. Osbert Sitwell was not the only poet to recall the Old Testament story of the elderly Abraham sacrificing his young son. Sitwell, who served with the Grenadier Guards, became disillusioned with the conduct of the war. Here he attacks the businessman who is making good profits out of the conflict and wants it to continue.

The Modern Abraham

His purple fingers clutch a large cigar –
  Plump, mottled fingers, with a ring or two.
He rests back in his fat armchair. The war
  Has made this change in him. As he looks through
His cheque-book with a tragic look he sighs:
  'Disabled Soldiers' Fund' he reads afresh,
And through his meat-red face peer angry eyes –
  The spirit piercing through its mound of flesh.
They should not ask me to subscribe again!
  Consider me and all that I have done –
I've fought for Britain with my might and main;
  I make explosives – and I gave a son.
My factory, converted for the fight
  (I do not like to boast of what I've spent),
Now manufactures gas and dynamite,
  Which only pays me seventy per cent.
And if I had ten other sons to send
I'd make them serve my country to the end,
So all the neighbours should flock round and say:
  'Oh! look what Mr Abraham has done.
He loves his country in the elder way;
  Poor gentleman, he's lost another son!'

OSBERT SITWELL

Which words suggest that this man has done well out of the war?
Which tell you that Sitwell hates him?
How has the man spent the war? In what ways has he 'fought for Britain'?
What does he value apart from money?
How does he consider the death of his son?
Is this poem comic or angry?

When Rudyard Kipling's only son was killed at Loos in 1915, he expressed his sorrow in a series of epigrams: brief, cleverly constructed poems, where much meaning is crammed into a few words. In two of these, he refers to the generation gap that so upset Sitwell and others.

Common Form

If any question why we died,
Tell them, because our fathers lied.

A Dead Statesman

I could not dig: I dared not rob:
Therefore I lied to please the mob.
Now all my lies are proved untrue
And I must face the men I slew.
What tale shall serve me here among
Mine angry and defrauded[1] young?

RUDYARD KIPLING

[1] cheated

Who is 'we' in the first poem?
What does 'our fathers lied' mean?
What is the purpose and point of this tiny poem?
In the second poem, why mention 'dig' and 'rob'?
What was the statesman good at?
What has happened to the statesman? Why does he now have to face the young?
Why are they 'angry and defrauded'?
What is Kipling saying about the war in these pieces?

In this cartoon by Will Dyson, Death comes to ask of the German Emperor, William II, 'Any orders today, Sire?'

'Grotesque' means strange or horribly distorted. It would be a good word to apply to Louis Golding's *The New Trade*. He worked with the Friends' (Quakers) Ambulance Service on various Fronts, and saw the effects of battle. He wrote many fiercely anti-war poems as a result of his experiences.

The New Trade

In the market-place they have made
A dolorous new trade.
Now you will see in the fierce naphtha[1] light.
Piled hideously to sight,
Dead limbs of men bronzed in the over-seas,
Bomb-wrenched from elbows and knees;
Torn feet that would, unwearied by harsh loads,
Have tramped steep moorland roads;
Torn hands that would have moulded exquisitely
Rare things for God to see;
And there are eyes there – blue like blue dove's wings,
Black like the Libyan kings,
Grey as before-dawn rivers, willow-stirred;
Brown as a nesting bird;
But all stare from the dark into the dark,
Reproachful, tense and stark.
Eyes heaped on trays and in broad baskets there,
Feet, hands and ropes of hair.
In the market-places . . . and women buy . . .
. . . Naphtha glares . . . hawkers cry . . .
Fat men rub hands
        . . . O God, O just God, send
Plagues, lightnings
        . . . make an end!

LOUIS GOLDING

[1] flare used to light market stalls

What is the point of this poem?
Which details do you find most grotesque?
Which people are the targets of Golding's anger here?
What does Golding find so tragic about war casualties?
What is the meaning of his last angry outburst?
How is this poem like and unlike *Of the Great White War*?

Alec Waugh fought in France and was taken prisoner. Here he looks at the death of a friend and the effects of this on himself and on people at home.

A French cartoon showing the Kaiser as a butcher dealing in the flesh of men killed on the Western Front

Cannon-fodder

Is it seven days you've been lying there
        Out in the cold,
Feeling the damp, chill circlet of flesh
        Loosen its hold
On muscles and sinews and bones,
        Feeling them slip
One from the other to hang, limp on the stones?
Seven days. The lice must be busy in your hair,
And by now the worms will have had their share
        Of eyelid and lip.
Poor, lonely thing; is death really a sleep?
Or can you somewhere feel the vermin creep
        Across your face
As you lie, rotting, uncared for in the unowned place,
That you fought so hard to keep
        Blow after weakening blow.
Well. You've got what you wanted, that spot is yours.
No one can take it from you now.

But at home by the fire, their faces aglow
        With talking of you,
They'll be sitting, the folk that you loved,
        And they will not know.

O Girl at the window combing your hair
    Get back to your bed.
    Your bright-limbed lover is lying out there
    Dead.

O mother, sewing by candlelight,
    Put away that stuff.
The clammy fingers of earth are about his neck.
    He is warm enough.

Soon, like a snake in your honest home
    The word will come.
And the light will suddenly go from it.
    Day will be dumb.
And the heart in each aching breast
    Will be cold and numb.

O men, who had known his manhood and truth,
    I had found him true.
O you, who had loved his laughter and youth,
    I had loved it too.
O girl, who has lost the meaning of life,
    I am lost as you.

And yet there is one worse thing,
For all the pain at the heart and the eye blurred and dim,
This you are spared,
You have not seen what death has made of him.

You have not seen the proud limbs mangled and
    broken,
The face of the lover sightless and raw and red,
You have not seen the flock of vermin swarming
    Over the newly dead.

Slowly he'll rot in the place where no man dare go,
Silently over the right the stench of his carcase will flow,
Proudly the worms will be banqueting . . .
    This you can never know.

He will live in your dreams for ever as last you saw him.
Proud-eyed and clean, a man whom shame never
    knew,
Laughing, erect, with the strength of the wind in his
    manhood –
    O broken-hearted mother, I envy you.

ALEC WAUGH

**What is horrifying about the first verse?
What is the force of his question, 'Is death
really a sleep?'
The soldier fought hard to stop the enemy
taking the ground where he was placed. What
is now so sad about that patch of ground?**

Gassed: *Gilbert Rogers*

people at home who
...er.
...will come 'like a snake'?
...o tell them about his dead

...poem he sees the people at
...kier than he is. Why exactly
...ror are they spared? What
...ind can they keep which the

...e plain, conversation-like style

...wn piece entitled *Cannon-fodder*.
...se the poem and picture to give
...deas.

W Read over the poems in this section. Write about some or all of them.
What are the targets for their anger?
What methods do the poets use in their writing to attack their targets?
Which poems are most successful?
What do you think of the poems and their subject-matter?

D Look over the illustrations in this section. Exactly what are the artists trying to say in each picture?
How do the pictures relate to the poems?
Which medium – words or drawing – is more forceful?

20 *Armistice and after*

The First World War ended by an Armistice at 11 a.m. on 11 November 1918. The tidy style of the eleventh hour of the eleventh day of the eleventh month appealed to the military mind of the time. A soldier remembered what it was like on that day at the Front when peace finally came.

> At a few minutes before eleven o'clock we all went to where the guns were, drawn up in a line behind a hedge. . . . All the guns fired. This was the first time I had heard our guns firing blank ammunition. The noise was no more than a bang, and puffs of white smoke hung over the muzzles of the guns and drifted slowly away. Some of the men started to cheer, but their voices sounded as unnatural as the noise of the guns, and they soon stopped. There was silence. It had come to stay . . .
>
> P.J. Campbell, *The Ebb and Flow of Battle*

Lord Dunsany was wounded at the Somme in 1916. His sonnet, *A Dirge of Victory*, shows no sense of pleasure or triumph at the defeat of Germany. A dirge is, in fact, a poem of sadness and mourning.

A Dirge of Victory

Lift not thy trumpet, Victory, to the sky,
  Nor through battalions nor by batteries blow,
  But over hollows full of old wire go,
Where, among dregs of war, the long-dead lie
With wasted iron that the guns passed by
  When they went eastward like a tide at flow;
  There blow thy trumpet that the dead may know,
Who waited for thy coming, Victory.

It is not we that have deserved thy wreath.
  They waited there among the towering weeds:
The deep mud burned under the thermite's[1] breath,
  And winter cracked the bones that no man heeds:
Hundreds of nights flamed by: the seasons passed.
And thou hast come to them at last, at last!

LORD DUNSANY

[1] explosive

Victory is often represented as a goddess blowing a trumpet of triumph.
Which people should she seek out and celebrate with at the war's end?
Who gave most to make victory possible?
Where are these people?
What is so sad about them?
Which line is most sad?
Do you find the word-pictures of the old battlefields impressive here?

May Cannan was working in a British government office in Paris when the war ended. She describes the atmosphere of this office when the news came through and the effect that the Armistice had on the girls working there.

The Armistice

The news came through over the telephone:
All the terms had been signed: the War was won:
And all the fighting and the agony,
And all the labour of the years were done.

One girl clicked sudden at her typewriter
And whispered, 'Jerry's safe,' and sat and stared:
One said, 'It's over, over, it's the end:
The War is over: ended': and a third,
'I can't remember life without the war'.
And one came in and said, 'Look here, they say
We can all go at five to celebrate,
As long as two stay on, just for today'.

It was quite quiet in the big empty room
Among the typewriters and little piles
Of index cards: one said, 'We'd better just
Finish the day's reports and do the files'.
And said, 'It's awf'lly like *Recessional*,[1]
Now when the tumult has all died away'.
The other said, 'Thank God we saw it through:
I wonder what they'll do at home today'.
And said, 'You know it will be quiet tonight
Up at the Front: first time in all these years,
And no one will be killed there any more',
And stopped, to hide her tears.
She said, 'I've told you; he was killed in June'.
The other said, 'My dear, I know; I know . . .
It's over for me too . . . My man was killed,
Wounded . . . and died . . . at Ypres . . . three years
  ago . . .
And he's my man, and I want him,' she said,
And knew that peace could not give back her dead.

MAY WEDDERBURN CANNAN

[1] poem by Rudyard Kipling

**Why does the writer not give any of the girls'
names?**
**What are their immediate reactions to the
news?**
**What are their later reactions, when the news
has sunk in?**
**This poem has real atmosphere. Which
details, especially of sounds, create this?**

'And knew that peace could not give back her dead'

George Willis served on the Western Front. In this extract from a long poem, he borrowed an idea from a recruiting poster showing a boy asking his father, 'What did you do in the Great War, Daddy?'

from: *Any Soldier to his Son*

What did I do, sonny, in the Great World War? –
Well, I learned to peel potatoes and to scrub the barrack
  floor . . .

I learned to ride as soldiers ride from Etaples to the
  Line,
For days and nights in cattle trucks, packed in like
  droves of swine . . . .
I learned to sleep by snatches on the fire step of a
  trench,
And to eat my breakfast mixed with mud and Fritz's
  heavy stench.
I learned to pray for Blighty ones[1] and lie and squirm
  with fear,
When Germans started strafing and the Blighty ones
  were near.

I learned to write home cheerful with my heart a lump
   of lead
With the thought of you and Mother, when she heard
   that I was dead . . .

So I learned to live and lump-it in the lovely land of war,
Where all the face of nature seems a monstrous septic
   sore,
Where all the bowels of earth hang open, like the guts of
   something slain,
And the rot and wreck of everything are churned and
   churned again;
Where all is done in darkness and where all is still in
   day,
Where living men are buried and the dead unburied lay;
Where men inhabit holes like rats, and only rats live
   there
Where cottage stood and castle once in days before La
   Guerre;
Where endless files of soldiers thread the everlasting
   way,
By endless miles of duckboards, through endless walls
   of clay;
Where life is one hard labour, and a soldier gets his rest
When they leave him in the daisies with a puncture in
   his chest;
Where still the lark in summer pours her warble from
   the skies,
And underneath, unheeding, lie the blank, upstaring
   eyes.

And I read the Blighty papers, where the warriors of the
   pen
Tell of 'Christmas in the Trenches' and 'The Spirit of our
   Men';
And I saved the choicest morsels and I read them to my
   chum,
And he muttered, as he cracked a louse and wiped it off
   his thumb:
'May a thousand chats[2] from Belgium crawl their
   fingers as they write;
May they dream they're not exempted till they faint
   with mortal fright;
May the fattest rats in Dickebusch[3] race over them in
   bed;
May the lies they've written choke them like a gas cloud
   till they're dead;
May the horror and the torture and the things they
   never tell
(For they only write to order) be reserved for them in
   Hell!'
You'd like to be a soldier and go to France some day?
By all the dead in Delville Wood[4], by all the nights I lay
Between our line and Fritz's before they brought me in;
By this old wood-and-leather stump, that once was
   flesh and skin:
By all the lads who crossed with me but never crossed
   again,

By all the prayers their mothers and their sweethearts
   prayed in vain,
Before the things that were that day should ever more
   befall
May God in common pity destroy us one and all!

GEORGE WILLIS

[1] a wound bad enough to send a man back to Britain

[2] lice

[3] near Ypres

[4] on the Somme, 1916

Willis describes the everyday horrors of the Great War soldier's life. Which details impress you most?
He then writes about 'Blighty (British) papers'. What various things do he and his friend resent about civilian journalists? What answer does Willis give to the boy when he claims that he would like to be a soldier?

W Imagine a conversation between son and father. The boy talks of the glamorous and glorious things that he has read about fighting; the father tells the truth. Keep close to the ideas in the poem.

W Imagine the day that peace came. You are perhaps a soldier, a civilian, or a nurse who has been through the war and survived. You go to a quiet place to reflect and to pick out various memories. What are they? Write about them.

In the first years after the war, Armistice Day was celebrated with careful ceremonial. The two minutes' silence was taken literally: traffic stopped and people stood still, bare-headed in the streets, remembering the dead. By 1921, the wartime industrial boom was over. As depression and unemployment grew, Prime Minister Lloyd George's promise 'to make Britain a fit country for heroes to live in' began to seem hollow. One ex-soldier recalled the problems of peace.

Although an expert machine-gunner, I was a numbskull so far as any trade or craft was concerned . . . and I joined the queues for jobs as messengers, window-cleaners and scullions. It was a complete let-down for thousands like me, and for some young officers, too. It was a common sight in London to see ex-officers with barrel-organs endeavouring to earn a living as beggars . . .

George Coppard, *With a Machine-gun to Cambrai*

Edward Shanks brings this disillusion into his poem about the Cenotaph ceremony.

Armistice Day 1921

The hush begins. Nothing is heard
Save the arrested taxi's throbbing
And here and there an ignorant bird
And here a sentimental woman sobbing.

The statesman bares and bows his head
Before the solemn monument;
His lips, paying duty to the dead
In silence, are more than ever eloquent.

But ere the sacred silence breaks
And taxis hurry on again,
A faint and distant voice awakes,
Speaking the mind of a million absent men:

'Mourn not for us. Our better luck
At least has given us peace and rest.
We struggled when our moment struck
But now we understand that death knew best.

'Would we be as our brothers are
Whose barrel-organs charm the town?
Ours was a better dodge by far –
We got *our* pensions in a lump sum down.

'We, out of all, have had our pay.
There is no poverty where we lie:
The graveyard has no quarter day,
The space is narrow but the rent not high.

'No empty stomach here is found;
Unless some cheated worm complain
You hear no grumbling underground:
O, never, never wish us back again!

'Mourn not for us, but rather we
Will meet upon this solemn day
And in our greater liberty
Keep silent for you, a little while, and pray.'

EDWARD SHANKS

**Shanks pretends to admire the statesman.
What does he really think?
Whose is the 'faint and distant voice'?
What does it say about the war dead and the survivors?
What is the grim joke in the last verse?**

W **Imagine a conversation between the statesman and the ex-soldier on the dole. Base it on the ideas from the poem.**

W **Study the still on the opposite page from the French anti-war film, *J'accuse*, made in the 1920s. In this scene, the war dead come alive again and leave their graves to come into town to see if their sacrifice in the fighting has been remembered and was worthwhile. Make a short story out of this idea.**

Survivors were haunted by their battle experiences for years. Modern psychologists recognize this state of delayed shock in war veterans but in 1918 men were left to manage as best they could. An Australian, Vance Palmer, served in France. He imagines a man who cannot forget the war, even when he returns, apparently unhurt, to his farm in the Australian bush.

The Farmer Remembers the Somme

Will they never fade or pass –
The mud, and the misty figures endlessly coming
In file through the foul morass,
And the grey flood-water lipping the reeds and grass,
And the steel wings drumming?

The hills are bright in the sun:
There's nothing changed or marred in the well-known
    places;
When work for the day is done
There's talk, and quiet laughter, and gleams of fun
On the old folks' faces.

I have returned to these;
The farm, and kindly Bush, and the young calves
    lowing;
But all that my mind sees
Is a quaking bog in a mist – stark, snapped trees,
And the dark Somme flowing.

VANCE PALMER

**Palmer sets two landscapes, of war and peace, beside each other.
How does one represent life and the other death?
Which key words create the mood of each?**

In *The Son*, Clifford Dyment shows a boy who lost his father in the war. One day, as he is growing up, he discovers an old letter written to his mother by the father he never knew. History suddenly comes alive to him.

Still from the French anti-war film of the 1920s, J'accuse

The Son

I found the letter in a cardboard box.
Unfamous history. I read the words.
The ink was frail and brown, the paper dry
After so many years of being kept.
The letter was a soldier's, from the front –
Conveyed his love and disappointed hope
Of getting leave. *It's cancelled now,* he wrote.
My luck is at the bottom of the sea.

Outside the sun was hot; the world looked bright;
I heard a radio, and someone laughed.
I did not sing, or laugh, or love the sun,
Within the quiet room I thought of him.
My father killed, and all the other men.
Whose luck was at the bottom of the sea.

CLIFFORD DYMENT

What is 'unfamous history'?
What effects does the letter have on the boy?
What does he learn from it that he has not understood before?
Why does he mention the 'hot sun', the 'bright world', the radio, the laugh?

W Write your own version of the boy's experience with the old letter: 'The day I found the letter'.

To conclude, read this poem written in 1915.

War

Over the World
Rages war.
Earth, sea and sky
Wince at his roar.

He tramples down
At every tread,
A million men,
A million dead.

We say that we
Must crush the Hun,
Or else the World
Will be undone.
But Huns are we
As much as they.
All men are Huns,
Who fight and slay.

And if we win,
And crush the Huns,
In twenty years
We must fight their sons,
Who will rise against
Our victory,
Their fathers', their own
Ignominy.[1]

And if their Kaiser
We dethrone,
They will his son restore,
Or some other one.
If we win by war,
War is a force,
And others to war
Will have recourse.

And through the World
Will rage new war.
Earth, sea and sky
Will wince at his roar.
He will trample down
At every tread,
Millions of men,
Millions of dead.

JOSEPH LEFTWICH

[1] disgrace

What is remarkable about this poem's general message?
What is uncanny about its details:
  We must fight their sons,
  Or some other one. . . .?
Why does the writer see war as pointless? Was he right?

Work based on poems from the whole of Part Two

W Referring closely to about six poems, write about one of the following.
  1 The picture of life on the Western Front as it is shown to us in these poems.
  2 The idea of the 'hero' in 1914-18 poetry.
  3 The gulf between civilians and fighting troops in the First World War.
  4 The reasons for the anger of First World War poets.

D Which two poems impressed you most? Prepare notes for a class discussion. It would be best to avoid such an obvious favourite as *Dulce et Decorum est*.

W Prepare an assembly reading by your class, which is based on a selection of First World War poems. You will need introductory material for the whole event and for individual poems.

D Hold a role-play discussion which is based on a meeting of a senior soldier, a politician, a civilian war-enthusiast, and a soldier from the Western Front. Try to bring in ideas from the poems.

PART 3

The Second World War and after

UNIT 21   *Glimpses of war: 1939 – 45*

Poetry was still a fashion in the Second World War. Memories of Owen and Sassoon made many men and women read and write poetry in the long periods of boredom between the violent episodes of the war. Most of this writing is about experience. There was little of the anger and satire of the First War: it was widely accepted that the struggles against the German Nazis and the Japanese were necessary and just.

We only watch, and indicate and make our scribbled
   pencil notes.
We do not wish to moralize, only to ease our dusty
   throats.

Donald Bain, from *War Poet*

Although there were remarkable poems and poets, somehow the poetry of the Second War does not make as great an impact as that of the First. It is the words of Wilfred Owen and others that create our mental picture of trench warfare. By 1939, however, other media – notably photography and film – had begun to replace the word in making the most vivid and lasting images of the Second War.

We can only include a few poems here which give us glimpses of people's lives and thoughts.

Air bombing meant that whole populations were involved in 'total war'. More civilians in Britain died than did members of the armed forces in battle. In a word-sketch, E.J. Scovell presents a picture of a mother's feelings before and after a German air-raid.

Days Drawing In

The days fail: night broods over afternoon:
And at my child's first drink beyond the night
Her skin is silver in the early light.
Sweet the grey morning and the raiders gone.

E.J. SCOVELL

Which words show the fear and tension of waiting for the German raids?
How does the poet show that the child is precious to the mother?
Which words express the relief at morning and survival?

Autumn Blitz

Unshaken world! Another day of light
After the human chaos of the night;
Although a heart in mendless horror grieves,
What calmly yellow, gently falling leaves!

FRANCES CORNFORD

What ideas are suggested by the phrase 'chaos of the night'?
What is the meaning of 'a heart in mendless horror grieves'?
What continues, surprisingly, throughout the bombing attack?

Chaos and destruction caused by bombing in London

Desmond Hawkins wrote an impression, based on real experience, of what he saw and heard in a London air raid shelter and on the streets as people waited for a German air-bombing attack during the London Blitz of 1940–41.

Night Raid

The sleepers humped down on the benches,
The daft boy was playing rummy with anyone he could
   get,
And the dancing girl said, 'What I say is,
If there's a bomb made for YOU,
You're going to get it.'
Someone muttered, 'The bees are coming again.'
Someone whispered beside me in the darkness,
'They're coming up from the east.'
Way off the guns muttered distantly.

This was in the small hours, at the ebb.
And the dancing girl clicked her teeth like castanets
And said, 'I don't mind life, believe me.
I like it. If there is any more to come,
I can take it and be glad of it.'
She was shivering and laughing and throwing her head
   back.
On the pavement men looked up thoughtfully,
Making plausible conjectures. The night sky
Throbbed under the cool bandage of the searchlights.

DESMOND HAWKINS

What is strange about the people in the shelter?
They react to danger in various ways: what are
these?
Which phrases create a sense of threat?
What might be the 'plausible conjectures' that

were made by the Air Raid Wardens and policemen on the street?

What does the comparison in the last lines tell you about the state of London during the bombing?

W Describe this odd and threatening experience in your own words, as a diary entry. Use the main ideas from the poem but add to the material from your own imagination.

The evacuation of schoolchildren from British cities began in September 1939. R.S. Thomas imagines a child's escape into the Welsh countryside after she has suffered the effects of the German Blitz on London.

The Evacuee

She woke up under a loose quilt
Of leaf patterns, woven by the light
At the small window, busy with the boughs
Of a young cherry; but wearily she lay,
Waiting for the siren, slow to trust
Nature's deceptive peace, and then afraid
Of the long silence, she would have crept
Uneasily from the bedroom with its frieze
Of fresh sunlight, had not a cock crowed,
Shattering the surface of that limpid pool
Of stillness, and before the ripples died
One by one in the field's shallows,
The farm woke with uninhibited din.

And now the noise and not the silence drew her
Down the bare stairs at great speed.
The sounds and voices were a rough sheet
Waiting to catch her, as though she leaped
From a scorched storey of the charred past.

And there the table and the gallery
Of farm faces trying to be kind
Beckoned her nearer, and she sat down
Under an awning of salt hams.

And so she grew, a small bird in the nest
Of welcome that was built about her,
Home now after so long away
In the flowerless streets of the drab town.
The men watched her busy with the hens,
The soft flesh ripening warm as corn
On the sticks of limbs, the grey eyes clear,
Rinsed with dew of their long dread.
The men watched her, and, nodding, smiled
With earth's charity, patient and strong.

R.S. THOMAS

What qualities of the farm are stressed in the first section of the poem?

What were the anxieties of the child in her old life?

Where does she think she is when she first wakes?

Explain the comparison about the 'rough sheet' in the second section.

How does the girl change physically and mentally as she stays on the farm?

The poem is a pattern of opposed ideas: pick out some of these. In particular, what is Thomas saying about city and country life? Do you like the many comparisons used here? Which impress you most?

W Write a story about the girl, describing her evacuation. Try to include her thoughts and the thoughts of those around her on the farm.

W Look at this photograph of evacuees, each labelled and holding a gas mask, preparing to leave London. Write your own evacuation story about one or several of the children.

Evacuees boarding a train at a London station, 1939

Soldiers of 1939–45 fought on battlegrounds across the world: in the desert of Libya, in the jungles of Burma, on Pacific islands, on Normandy beaches, on Greek islands. Aircraft and tanks made battles more open and rapidly moving, and so prevented too many stagnant trench war situations from developing. There may have been less anger about poor leadership but the pity of war, in its effects on the individual, remained the key theme of soldiers' poetry and prose-writing.

John Masefield wrote a set of poems about all kinds of people who were caught up in war. This is about a soldier saying goodbye at a station.

Mother and Son

He sees his comrades, and a coming test
In which he hopes to shine, not yet perceiving
How mud may soil a fallen Hector's[1] crest,
And Priam's[2] palace echo with girls grieving.

She only sees her son, her life's one star,
The leaping little lad of days that were,
Somewhere alone amid the wreck of war,
Crying for help from her and she not there.

                    JOHN MASEFIELD

[1] Greek prince killed in Trojan War story
[2] Hector's father and King of Troy

What is the young soldier thinking about as he leaves for war?
What does the poet know about the fate of soldiers?
What does the mother think about as she says goodbye?
Find out more about Hector and Priam so that you can see the point of the reference.

In *Route March Rest*, Vernon Scannell is looking back on his war service after half a century. He imagines a moment of peace in war, as tired marching soldiers rest in a village. Soon they will go overseas to fight.

Route March Rest

They marched in staggered columns through the lanes
Drowsy with dust and summer, rifles slung.
All other-ranks wore helmets and the sun
Drummed on bobbing metal plates and purred
Inside their skulls; the thumping tramp of boots
On gravel crunched. B Company had become

A long machine that clanked and throbbed. The reek
Of leather, sweat and rifle-oil was thick
And khaki on the body of the day.
All dainty fragrances were shouldered out
Though thrush and blackbird song could not be stilled
And teased some favoured regions of the air.

They reached a village and the order came
To halt and fall out for a rest. The men
Unslung their rifles, lit up cigarettes,
And sprawled or squatted on the village green.
Opposite the green, next to the church,
The school, whose open windows with wild flowers
In glass jars on the sills framed pools of dark,
Was silent, cool; but from the playground sprayed
The calls of children, bright as buttercups,
Until a handbell called them in from play
And then B Company was ordered back
To fall in on the road in their platoons
And start the march again.
                    Beyond the church
They passed a marble plinth and saw the roll
Of names, too many surely for this small
Community, and as the files trudged on,
Faintly from the school, like breath of flowers
But half-remembered, children's voices rose:
'All things bright and beautiful,' they sang,
Frail sound, already fading, soon to die.

                    VERNON SCANNELL

This is a poem of contrasts, rather like Owen's *Spring Offensive*.
What features of the marching soldiers contrast with their surroundings in the summer countryside?
The men rest by the village school. How are they like or unlike the children?
What thoughts come to the men as they look at the school and the pupils?
What is the 'marble plinth' with its 'roll of names'?
What effect does this plinth have on the soldiers' thoughts?
What two meanings has 'soon to die' in the last line?
What sad ideas are there in the last four lines?

Keith Douglas is often thought of as the Wilfred Owen of the Second World War. He fought against the Germans and Italians in the Libyan desert, and was killed during the invasion of Normandy in 1944.

Here he writes about a dead German who was found after a desert battle.

I looked down into the face of a man lying hunched up in a pit. His expression of agony seemed so acute and urgent, his stare so wild and despairing, that for a moment I thought him alive. He was like a cleverly posed waxwork. . . . The dust which powdered his face like an actor's lay on his wide open eyes. . . . This picture, as they say, told a story. It filled me with useless pity.

Keith Douglas, *Alamein to Zem-Zem*

Vergissmeinnicht[1]

Three weeks gone and the combatants gone
returning over the nightmare ground
we found the place again, and found
the soldier sprawling in the sun.

The frowning barrel of his gun
overshadowing. As we came on
that day, he hit my tank with one
like the entry of a demon.

Look. Here in the gunpit spoil
the dishonoured picture of his girl
who has put: *Steffi. Vergissmeinnicht*
in a copybook gothic script.

We see him almost with content,
abased, and seeming to have paid
and mocked at by his own equipment
that's hard and good when he's decayed.

But she would weep to see today
how on his skin the swart flies move;
the dust upon the paper eye
and the burst stomach like a cave.

For here the lover and killer are mingled
who had one body and one heart.
And death who had the soldier singled
has done the lover mortal hurt.

KEITH DOUGLAS

[1] 'Do not forget me'

What is sad about the material scattered around the dead man?
What two aspects of human life does Douglas see in the German?
What would the man's girlfriend be shocked at?

Dead German on the Hitler line, Italy: Charles Comfort

Louis Simpson fought with the American Army at the Normandy landings of 1944 and across Europe afterwards. Here he writes about an incident in the Ardennes, scene of a heavy German counter-attack during the winter of 1944–5.

The Battle

Helmet and rifle, pack and overcoat
Marched through a forest. Somewhere up ahead
Guns thudded. Like the circle of a throat
The night on every side was turning red.

They halted and they dug. They sank like moles
Into the clammy earth between the trees.
And soon the sentries, standing in their holes,
Felt the first snow. Their feet began to freeze.

At dawn the first shell landed with a crack.
Then shells and bullets swept the icy woods.
This lasted many days. The snow was black.
The corpses stiffened in their scarlet hoods.

Most clearly of that battle I remember
The tiredness in eyes, how hands looked thin
Around a cigarette, and the bright ember
Would pulse with all the life there was within.

LOUIS SIMPSON

Why does the poet not mention a person in the first two lines, only the things that a person carries?

What comparison is used to describe the battle line as the men approach it?
What are the worst aspects of this winter war?
The scene is black and white. What provides the only colour?
The last verse mentions an individual soldier. What is pathetic about him?
What does the glowing cigarette seem to represent in the last two lines?

Randall Jarrell served with the US Air Force. This poem is a general picture of the ordinary private soldier of the Second World War, but he could be a man from any war in history.

A Lullaby

For wars his life and half a world away
The soldier sells his family and days.
He learns to fight for freedom and the State;
He sleeps with seven men within six feet.

He picks up matches and he cleans out plates;
Is lied to like a child, cursed like a beast.
They crop his head, his dog tags ring like sheep
As his stiff limbs shift wearily to sleep.

Recalled in dreams or letters, else forgot,
His life is smothered like a grave with dirt;
And his dull torment mottles like a fly's
The lying amber of the histories.

RANDALL JARRELL

The 'dull torment' of the soldier's life: Canadian troops in Holland 1944-5, painted by Alex Colville

What does he give up to fight?
What are the worst aspects of his life and work?
How is he treated?
Why is his fighting for freedom a grim kind of joke?
How is he remembered when he dies?
He is trapped in history as a fly is sometimes caught and preserved in amber.
Why is history called 'lying amber'?

Look over all of these poems about the Second World War.

D Discuss whether or not they are as impressive and interesting as those of the First War. Give careful reasons for your argument.

W Write about some or all of these poems. What do they tell us about life, about the thoughts and feelings of civilians and soldiers?
What do you find moving, strange, or interesting about their content and about the way in which they are written?

UNIT 22   *The shadow of the Bomb*

A new kind of war began on 6 August 1945, when the first atomic bomb exploded over Hiroshima in Japan. It destroyed a whole city, killing 60 000 people at once and injuring 100 000 others, many of whom died later of radiation sickness. The Americans dropped a second bomb on Nagasaki on 9 August to end the Second World War and to begin the nuclear age.

Hiroshima after the atomic bomb, August 1945

The first instant was pure light, blinding, intense light, but light of an awesome beauty and variety. . . . If there was sound, no one heard it. The initial flash spawned a succession of calamities. First came heat. It lasted only an instant but was so intense that it melted roof tiles, fused the quartz crystals in granite blocks, charred the exposed sides of telephone poles for almost two miles, and incinerated nearby humans, so thoroughly that nothing remained except their shadows, burned into the asphalt pavements or stone walls. . . . Bare skin was burned up to two and a half miles away. After the heat came the blast, sweeping outward from the fireball with the force of a five-hundred-mile-an-hour wind . . . in a giant circle more than two miles across, everything was reduced to rubble.

F. Knebel and C. Bailey, *No High Ground*

Beach girl: nuclear victim, *a fibre-glass sculpture: Colin Self*

Hiroshima was too vast, too remote, too shocking a horror for most people to understand. Here is one tiny comment. (Albert Einstein was one of the scientists who discovered the principles that led to the invention of the atomic bomb.)

Relative Sadness

Einstein's eyes
were filled with tears
when he heard about Hiroshima.

Mr. Tamihi
had no eyes left
to show his grief.

COLIN ROWBOTHAM

This poem is written in the concise style of some Japanese poetry. What point is the author making in his title and in his contrast of Einstein and Mr Tamihi, an ordinary Japanese?
Do you think that the scientists who thought out the principles of the Bomb should have concealed their discoveries?

Edwin Muir wrote indirectly about nuclear war in *The Horses*, which the poet T.S. Eliot called 'that great, that terrifying poem of the atomic age'. Muir imagines a final war which causes the collapse of machine-dominated civilization. Only a few people, such as the Scottish islanders in the poem, manage to survive.

The Horses

Barely a twelvemonth after
The seven days war that put the world to sleep,
Late in the evening the strange horses came.
By then we had made our covenant with silence
But in the first few days it was so still
We listened to our breathing and were afraid.
On the second day
The radios failed; we turned the knobs; no answer.
On the third day a warship passed us, heading north,
Dead bodies piled on the deck. On the sixth day
A plane plunged over us into the sea. Thereafter
Nothing. The radios dumb:
And still they stand in corners of our kitchens,
And stand, perhaps, turned on, in a million rooms
All over the world. But now if they should speak,
If on a sudden they should speak again,
If on the stroke of noon a voice should speak,
We would not listen, we would not let it bring
That bad old world that swallowed its children quick
At one great gulp. We would not have it again.
Sometimes we think of the nations lying asleep,
Curled blindly in impenetrable sorrow,
And then the thought confounds us with its
    strangeness.

The tractors lie about our fields; at evening
They look like dank sea-monsters crouched and
    waiting.
We leave them where they are and let them rust:
'They'll moulder away and be like other loam.'
We make our oxen drag our rusty ploughs,
Long laid aside. We have gone back
Far past our fathers' land.
                    And then, that evening
Late in the summer the strange horses came.
We heard a distant tapping on the road,
A deepening drumming; it stopped, went on again,
And at the corner changed to hollow thunder.
We saw the heads
Like a wild wave charging and were afraid.

We had sold our horses in our fathers' time
To buy new tractors. Now they were strange to us
As fabulous steeds set on an ancient shield
Or illustrations in a book of knights.
We did not dare go near them. Yet they waited,
Stubborn and shy, as if they had been sent
By an old command to find our whereabouts
And that long-lost archaic companionship.
In the first moment we had never a thought
That they were creatures to be owned and used.
Among them were some half-a-dozen colts
Dropped in some wilderness of the broken world,
Yet new as if they had come from their own Eden.
Since then they have pulled our ploughs and borne our
    loads,
But that free servitude still can pierce our hearts.
Our life is changed; their coming our beginning.

EDWIN MUIR

What signs of the war and its effects do the islanders notice?
What is a strange feature of the new way of life (lines 4-6)?
How do the people now feel about machines?
What does 'far past our fathers' land' mean?
'The seven days war' reminds us of God's creation of the world in that time, as told in the Book of Genesis. Now He destroys it in seven days. Why is God angry with Man?
The horses appear magically on the island, presumably sent by God.
Why has He sent them?
What does 'that long-lost archaic relationship' mean?
Why is the islanders' contact with the horses superior to their former reliance on machines?
What, then, is the theme, or general idea, of the poem?
What does it tell us about Man and Science in the nuclear age?

W Imagine that you are one of the islanders. Write, as a set of diary entries or a short story, about your experiences during and after the war. Include the arrival of the horses. Your writing should make clear the meaning of the horses in helping to create a new and simpler civilization.

American nuclear test explosion in the Pacific, 1945

The vastly increased power of nuclear weapons that have been developed since 1945 and the large stockpiles of such bombs that are now held by major world powers have aroused fears that a Third World War would end life on earth.

Adrian Mitchell is a leading protest poet whose main weapon is his chilling black humour. He sees governments as engaged in sinister plots against ordinary people. One of his poems, called *I Was Walking*, begins

I was walking in a government warehouse
Where the daylight never goes.
I saw fifteen million plastic bags
Hanging in a thousand rows . . .

The bags are for the future victims of nuclear war. Mitchell returns to this idea in another poem, *Appendix IV*. He has been reading a Civil Defence manual about what to do in the event of war.

'Appendix IV Requirements in the shelter

    Clothing
    Cooking equipment
    Food
    Furniture
    Hygiene
    Lighting
    Medical
    Shrouds'
What
    'Shrouds.
    Several large, strong black plastic bags
    and a reel of 2-inch, or wider, adhesive tape
    can make adequate airtight containers for deceased
    persons until the situation permits burial.'

No I will not put my lovely wife into a large strong black
   plastic bag
No I will not put my lovely children into large strong

black plastic bags
No I will not put my lovely dog or my lovely cats into
 large strong black plastic bags
I will embrace them all until I am filled with their
 radiation
Then I will carry them, one by one,
Through the black landscape
And lay them gently at the concrete door
Of the concrete block
Where the colonels
And the chief detectives
And the MPs
And the Regional Commissioners
Are biding their time

And then I will lie down with my wife and children
And my dog and cats

And we will wait for the door to open.

ADRIAN MITCHELL

Why does he hate the instructions?
What does he intend to do with his dead
family?
Who seem to be the enemies of ordinary
people?
How have they protected themselves?
Do you think that the anger and black
humour of the poem make an effective
protest?

Roger McGough also uses an apparently comic
style to write about nuclear disaster. He imagines
that a meteorite sets off the warning system
against nuclear attack from the Russians. The
Americans immediately launch a massive counter-
attack.

Icarus Allsorts

'A meteorite is reported to have landed
in New England. No damage is said . . .'

A littlebit of heaven fell
From out the sky one day
It landed in the ocean
Not so very far away
The General at the radar screen
Rubbed his hands with glee
And grinning pressed the button
That started World War Three.

From every corner of the earth
Bombs began to fly
There were even missile jams

No traffic lights in the sky
In the time it takes to blow your nose
The people fell, the mushrooms rose

'House!' cried the fatlady
As the bingohall moved to various parts of the town

'Raus!' cried the German butcher
as his shop came tumbling down

Philip was in the countinghouse
Counting out his money
The Queen was in the parlour
Eating bread and honey

When through the window
Flew a bomb
And made them go all funny

In the time it takes to draw a breath
Or eat a toadstool, instant death

The rich
Huddled outside the doors of their fallout shelters
Like drunken carolsingers

The poor
Clutching shattered televisions
And last week's editions of T.V. Times
(but the very last)

Civil defence volunteers
With their tin hats in one hand
And their heads in the other

C.N.D. supporters
Their ban the bomb badges beginning to rust
Have scrawled 'I told you so' in the dust.

A littlebit of heaven fell
From out the sky one day
It landed in Vermont
North-Eastern U.S.A.
The general at the radar screen
He should have got the sack
But that wouldn't bring
Three thousand million, seven hundred, and sixty-
 eight people back,
Would it?

ROGER McGOUGH

There are many grim jokes in this poem.
Are there any serious points in it?
Would you say that this is a good way to write
about the danger of nuclear war?

W Write your own protest poem against nuclear war. Think, perhaps, of everything that you love – family, home, countryside, cities, wild life, natural beauty – that would be destroyed by it.

W Look at this still from *The War Game*, a film about the consequences of nuclear war. Use it as the basis of your own story called 'The day the Bomb dropped'.

Still from the anti-nuclear film, **The War Game**

FURTHER READING

First World War

Background

The First World War: An Illustrated History, A.J.P. Taylor,
    Penguin
The First World War, A. Brown, Wayland
The Battle of the Somme, C. Martin, Wayland
World War I, R. Hoare, Macdonald
The First World War, J. Pimlott, Franklin Watts

Poetry

Poetry of the Great War, D. Hibberd and J. Onions,
    Macmillan
    The best of many collections.
The War Poets, R. Giddings, Bloomsbury
    Well illustrated collection and comment.
The War Poets, C. Martin, Wayland
    Brief illustrated biographies of Brooke, Sassoon,
    Owen, Rosenberg.
Poetry of the First World War, E. Hudson, Wayland
    Poems and photographs.
Scars upon the Heart, C. Reilly, Virago
    Women's verse of the war.
The English Poets of the First World War, J. Lehmann,
    Thames and Hudson
British Poets of the First World War, F. Crawford,
    Associated Universities Press
    Clear, useful critical comments on poets and poems.

Owen and Sassoon

The Poems of Wilfred Owen, J. Stallworthy (ed.), Hogarth
    Press
Wilfred Owen (biography), J. Stallworthy, Oxford
    University Press
Selected Letters of Wilfred Owen, J. Bell (ed.), Oxford
    University Press
The War Poems, (collected edition of Sassoon's pieces on
    the war) Faber
Diaries 1915-19: Faber
Memoirs of a Fox-Hunting Man: Faber
Memoirs of an Infantry Officer: Faber
Sherston's Progress: Faber
    Semi-autobiographical account: Sassoon writes of
        himself as George Sherston.
The Pity of War: The Meeting of Owen and Sassoon: video,
    Oxford Vision

Wide reading

Goodbye to All That, Robert Graves, Penguin Modern
    Classics
    The Battle of Loos 1915 and the Somme 1916.
Undertones of War, Edmund Blunden, Penguin Modern
    Classics

The Somme 1916 and Ypres 1917.
Her Privates We, Frederic Manning, Pan
    Vivid novel about soldiers on the Somme.
With a Machine-gun to Cambrai, G. Coppard, HMSO
    A private soldier's memories.
Strange Meeting, Susan Hill, Longman
    Story of two friends involved in the war.
All Quiet on the Western Front, Erich Remarque,
    Heinemann
    Famous German anti-war novel of the late 1920s.
Under Fire, Henri Barbusse, Dent Everyman
    French war novel from 1917 that impressed Sassoon
    and Owen.
No Hero for the Kaiser, R. Frank, Swallow.
    German anti-war novel banned by Hitler, and
    recently re-discovered.
Testament of Youth, Vera Brittain, Virago
Chronicle of Youth, Vera Brittain, Gollancz
    A wartime VAD nurse describes the suffering that
    she saw in the war.
Diary Without Dates, Enid Bagnold, Virago
    Another nurse's view of the victims of war.

Second World War

Background

The Second World War, M. Pierre, Wayland
Spotlight on the Second World War, N. Harris, Wayland

Poetry

The Terrible Rain, B. Gardner (ed.), Methuen
    War poems of World War II.
Chaos of the Night, C. Reilly, Virago
    War poems by British women.

Wide reading

Alamein to Zem-Zem, Keith Douglas, Penguin Modern
    Classics
    The war poet's picture of battle in the Libyan desert.
Going Solo, Roald Dahl, Heinemann
    Fine picture of the air war over Greece.
Vessel of Sadness, William Woodruff, Chatto/Dent
    Brilliant study of soldiers at Anzio in Italy.
Fleshwounds, David Holbrook, Methuen
    A novel that contains a gripping picture of D-Day and
    fighting in Normandy in 1944.
The Long and the Short and the Tall, Willis Hall,
    Heinemann
    Powerful play about men fighting in Malaya.
Hiroshima, John Hersey, Penguin Modern Classics
    The true story of what happened on the day of the
    Bomb, told by several survivors.

INDEX OF POETS

INDEX OF TITLES

─────── INDEX OF FIRST LINES ───────

POETS AND POEMS

A.E. Housman 1859-1936   *On the Idle Hill*
Maurice Hewlett 1861-1923   *For Two Voices*
S.T.Coleridge 1772-1834   from *Fears in Solitude*
John Scott 1730-1783   *The Drum*
Robert Southey 1774-1843   *The Battle of Blenheim*
Lord Byron 1788-1824   from *Childe Harold's Pilgrimage*
Rainer Maria Rilke 1875-1926   *Before Waterloo*,
   translated by Robert Lowell 1917-77, 'Imitations':
   Faber 1962
Alfred Tennyson 1809-1892   *The Charge of the Light
   Brigade*
Walt Whitman 1819-1892   *Come up from the Fields Father*
Bret Harte 1836-1902   *What the Bullet Sang*
Henry Newbolt 1862-1938   *Vitai Lampada*
Thomas Hardy 1840-1928   *Drummer Hodge*
B. Paul Neuman   *Vox Militantis*
Thomas Hardy 1840-1928   *A Wife in London*
Edgar Wallace 1875-1932   *War*
Rudyard Kipling 1865-1936   *Dirge of the Dead Sisters*
                            The Hyaenas
William Watson 1858-1935   from *The World in Armour*
Thomas Hardy 1840-1928   *Channel Firing*
John Peale Bishop 1892-1944   from *In the Dordogne*,
   'Selected poems': Chatto and Windus 1960
Gilbert Frankau 1884-1952   from *The Guns*, 'Poetical
   Works I': Chatto and Windus 1923
Siegfried Sassoon 1886-1967   from *Prelude: The Troops*,
   'Counter-Attack': Heinemann 1918
Harold Begbie 1871-1929   *Fall In*
Matilda Betham-Edwards 1836-1919   *Two Mothers*
Jessie Pope 1868-1941   *Who's for the Game?*, 'Jessie
   Pope's War Poems': Grant Richards 1915
E.A. Mackintosh 1893-1917   *Recruiting*
Herbert Asquith 1881-1947   *The Volunteer*, 'Poems
   1912-33': Sidgwick and Jackson 1934
Rupert Brooke 1887-1915   *Peace*
Katherine Tynan 1861-1931   *To the Others*
John McCrae 1872-1918   *In Flanders Fields*
Laurence Binyon 1869-1943   from *For the Fallen*,
   'Laurence Binyon Anthology': Hodder and
   Stoughton 1927
Robert Nichols 1893-1944   *Dawn on the Somme*,
'Ardours and Endurances': Chatto and Windus 1917
Robert Graves 1895-1985   *A Dead Boche*, 'Poems
   1914-26': Heinemann 1927
Ruth Comfort Mitchell 1882-1953   *He went for a Soldier*,
   'Poems of the Great War': Macmillan NY 1916
Hugh Freston 1892-1916   from *O Fortunati*
Arthur Graeme West 1891-1917   *God! How I hate you*
Gilbert Frankau 1884-1952   from *The Other Side*,
   'Poetical Works II': Chatto and Windus 1923
Siegfried Sassoon 1886-1967 from *Counter-Attack*,
   'Counter-Attack': Heinemann 1918
Robert Nichols 1893-1944   *Comrades: an Episode*,
   'Ardours and Endurances': Chatto and Windus 1917

Wilfred Owen 1893-1918   *Spring Offensive*
Julian Grenfell 1888-1915   *Into Battle*
Wilfred Owen 1893-1918   *Exposure*
Edgell Rickword 1898-1982   *Winter Warfare*, 'Collected
   Poems': John Lane 1947
Wilfred Owen 1893-1918   *Disabled*
Siegfried Sassoon 1886-1967   *The General*, 'Counter-
   Attack': Heinemann 1918
A.P. Herbert 1890-1971   *After the Battle*, 'The Bomber
   Gipsy': Methuen 1919
Godfrey Elton 1892-1973   *The Survivor*, 'Years of
   Peace': Allen and Unwin 1925
Herbert Asquith 1881-1947   *The Fallen Subaltern*,
   'Poems 1912-33': Sidgwick and Jackson 1934
Wilfred Owen 1893-1918   *Futility*
Siegfried Sassoon 1886-1967   *Died of Wounds*, 'The Old
   Huntsman': Heinemann 1917
   The Hero, 'The Old Huntsman': Heinemann 1917
   Base Details, 'Counter-Attack': Heinemann 1918
   Suicide in the Trenches, 'Counter-Attack': Heinemann
   1918
   Does it Matter? 'Counter-Attack,: Heinemann 1918
   Great Men, 'The War Poems': Faber 1983
Wilfred Owen 1893-1918
   from *The Ballad of Peace and War*
   Anthem for Doomed Youth
   Dulce et Decorum est
W.N. Ewer 1885-1976   *Five Souls*, 'Five Souls and other
   wartime verses': The Herald/The Pelican Press 1917
Harold Begbie 1871-1929   *War Exults*
H. Smalley Sarson   *The Shell*
Israel Zangwill 1864-1926   *1916*
Wilfrid Gibson 1878-1962   *The Conscript*, 'Collected
   Poems 1905-25': Macmillan 1926
Thomas Burke 1886-1945   *Of the Great White War*, 'The
   Songbook of Quong Lee of Limehouse': Allen and
   Unwin 1920
Osbert Sitwell 1892-1969   *The Modern Abraham*,
   'Selected Poems Old and New': Duckworth 1943
Rudyard Kipling 1865-1936   *Common Form*
                            A Dead Statesman
Louis Golding 1895-1958   *The New Trade*, 'Sorrow
   of War': Methuen 1919
Alec Waugh 1898-1981   *Cannon-fodder*, 'Resentment:
   poems': Grant Richards 1918
Lord Dunsany 1878-1957   *A Dirge of Victory*, 'Fifty
   Poems': Putnam 1929
May Wedderburn Cannan 1893-1973   *The Armistice*, 'In
   Wartime': Longmans Green 1917
George Willis   from *Any Soldier to his Son*, 'Any
   Soldier to his Son': Allen and Unwin 1919
Edward Shanks 1892-1953   *Armistice Day 1921*,
   'Poems 1912-32': Macmillan 1933
Vance Palmer 1885-1959   *The Farmer Remembers the
   Somme*, 'The Camp': Sydney J. Endacott (Australia)
   1920

Clifford Dyment 1914- *The Son*, 'Poems 1935-48': Dent 1970

Joseph Leftwich 1892-1983 *War*, 'Along the Years': Auscombe and Co. 1937

Donald Bain 1922- from *War Poet*, 'Penguin New Writing 21': Penguin 1944

E.J. Scovell 1907- *Days Drawing In*, 'The First Year': Cresset Press 1940

Frances Cornford 1886-1960 *Autumn Blitz*, 'Travelling Home': Cresset Press 1948

Desmond Hawkins 1908- *Night Raid*, 'Poetry in Wartime': Faber 1942

R.S. Thomas 1913- *The Evacuee*, 'Song at the Year's Turning': Granada 1956

John Masefield 1878-1967 *Mother and Son*, 'A Generation Risen': Collins 1942

Vernon Scannell 1922- *Route March Rest*, 'Soldiering On': Robson Books 1989

Keith Douglas 1920-1944 *Vergissmeinnicht*, 'Selected Poems': Faber 1964

Louis Simpson 1923- *The Battle*, 'Selected Poems': Oxford 1966

Randall Jarrell 1914-1965 *A Lullaby*, 'Complete Poems': Faber 1971

Colin Rowbotham *Relative Sadness*, 'Touchstones 5': Hodder and Stoughton 1971

Edwin Muir 1887-1959 *The Horses*, 'Collected Poems': Faber 1958

Adrian Mitchell 1932- from *Fifteen Million Plastic Bags*, 'Poems 1964': Cape 1966

Appendix IV: Requirements in the Shelter, 'On the Beach at Cambridge': Allison and Busby 1984

Roger McGough 1937- *Icarus Allsorts*, 'The Mersey Sound': Penguin 1967

Note

Wilfred Owen poems: texts from 'The Complete Poems and Fragments', J. Stallworthy (ed.): Oxford/Chatto 1983

ACKNOWLEDGEMENTS

The editor and publisher would like to thank the following for permission to reproduce poems:

'Before Waterloo, the Last Night' by Robert Lowell, reprinted by permission of Faber and Faber Ltd from *History*; The Estate of Gilbert Frankau for 'The Other Side' from *Poetical Works II*, by permission of Chatto & Windus; Sidgwick and Jackson Limited for 'The Volunteer' and 'The Fallen Subaltern' by Herbert Asquith from *Poems 1912–33*; The Literary Estate of Robert Nichols for 'Dawn on the Somme' and 'Comrades' from *Ardours and Endurances*, by permission of Chatto & Windus; A P Watt Limited on behalf of the Executors of the Estate of Robert Graves for 'A Dead Boche' from *Poems About War*; Mr Willian Sanborn Young for 'He Went for a Soldier' by Ruth Comfort Mitchell from *Poems of the Great War*; Crystal Hale and Jocelyn Herbert for 'After the Battle' from *The Bomber Gipsy* by A P Herbert, by permission of A P Watt Ltd, Literary Agents; Mr George T Sassoon for 'Counter Attack', 'The General', 'Base Details', 'Suicide in the Trenches' by Siegfried Sassoon from *Counter Attack* and for 'Died of Wounds' and 'The Hero' by Siegfried Sassoon from *The Old Huntsman* and for 'Great Men' by Siegfried Sassoon, from *The War Poems*; Mr Michael Gibson for 'The Conscript' by W W Gibson from *Collected Poems 1905–25*, by permission of Macmillan, London and Basingstoke; Duckworth and Co Ltd. for 'The Modern Abraham' by Osbert Sitwell from *Selected Poems Old and New*, by permission of David Higham Associates Ltd; Methuen and Co. for 'The New Trade' by Louis Golding from *Sorrow of War*; The Bodley Head for 'A Dirge of Victory' by Lord Dunsany from *Fifty Poems*; Mr J C Slater for 'The Armistice' by May Wedderburn Cannan from *The Splendid Days*; Macmillan, London and Basingstoke for 'Armistice Day' by Edward Shanks from *Poems 1912–32*; Clifford Dyment for 'The Son' from *Poems 1935–48*, by permission of J M Dent & Sons; Carcanet Press Limited for 'Days Drawing In' by E J Scovell from *Collected Poems*; Barrie and Jenkins for 'Autumn Blitz' from *Travelling Home* by Frances Cornford, The Cresset Press, 1948, reprinted by permission; Desmond Hawkins for 'Night Raid' from *Poetry in Wartime* by permission of David Higham Associates Ltd; Gwydion Thomas for 'The Evacuee' by R S Thomas from *Song at the Year's Turning*; The Society of Authors as the literary representative of the Estate of John Masefield for 'Mother and Son' from *A Generation Risen*; 'Vergissmeinnicht' © Marie J Douglas 1978. Reprinted from *The Complete Poems of Keith Douglas* edited by Desmond Graham (1978) by permission of Oxford University Press; Louis Simpson for 'The Battle' from *Selected Poems*; 'A Lullaby' by Randall Jarrell, reprinted by permission of Faber and Faber Ltd from *The Complete Poems*; Colin Rowbotham for 'Relative Sadness' from *Touchstones 5*; 'The Horses' by Edwin Muir reprinted by permission of Faber and Faber Ltd from *The Collected Poems of Edwin Muir*; 'Icarus Allsorts' by Roger McGough from *Modern Poets 10 – The Mersey Sound*, by permission of the Peters Fraser & Dunlop Group Ltd; Adrian Mitchell for 'Fifteen Million Plastic Bags : Appendix IV: Requirements in the Shelter' from *Poems 1964*, by permission of Allison & Busby.

Whilst every effort has been made to contact the copyright-holders, this has not proved to be possible in every case.

The editor and publisher would like to thank the following for permission to reproduce illustrative material. (The numbers given are page numbers.)

Barnaby's Picture Library: 74; The Bettmann Archive, Hulton-Deutsch Collection: 85; British Museum: 42, 43 (top and bottom), 56, 62, 63, 65; By permission of the Syndics of Cambridge University Library: 11, 51, 67, 69 (left and right), 70; Canadian War Museum: 84; Collections Musée Royal de l'Armée, Bruxelles: 71; Design and Artists Copyright Society © Colin Self 1989, All Rights Reserved DACS: 86; Gemäldegalerie Neue Meister – Staatliche Kunstsammlungen Dresden: 25; The Mansell Collection Limited: 68; Mary Evans Picture Library: 10, 53 (right); Fitzwilliam Museum, Cambridge: 57; Hulton-Deutsch Collection: 7 (top and bottom), 16 (top and bottom), 23, 34, 81, 88; Illustrated London News Picture Library: 38; Imperial War Museum: cover, 8 (top), 27, 29 (top and bottom), 30, 31, 33, 35 (four pictures), 39, 45, 50, 53 (left), 55, 58, 59, 64, 72, 80; Professor Dr. Arne A Kollwitz: 8 (bottom); Landesmuseum, Brunswick: 14; Leeds City Art Gallery: 6 (top); National Army Museum, London: 19; National Film Archive: 77, 90; National Museum of Canada: 83; National Portrait Gallery: 66 (top); Southampton Art Gallery: 28; The Tate Gallery, London and Luke Gertler: 66 (bottom); Wayland (Publishers) Limited: 21; Wellcome Institute Library, London: 6 (bottom).